MIKE THE BI

THE STORY OF MIKE HAIL W

Also from Veloce Publishing ...

Enthusiast's Restoration Manual Series
Ducati Bevel Twins 1971 to 1986 (Falloon)
How to restore Honda CX500 & CX650 – YOUR
   step-by-step colour illustrated guide to complete
   restoration (Burns)
How to restore Honda Fours – YOUR step-by-step colour
   illustrated guide to complete restoration (Burns)
Triumph Trident T150/T160 & BSA Rocket III, How to
   Restore (Rooke)

Essential Buyer's Guide Series
BMW Boxer Twins (Henshaw)
BMW GS (Henshaw)
BSA 350, 441 & 500 Singles (Henshaw)
BSA 500 & 650 Twins (Henshaw)
BSA Bantam (Henshaw)
Ducati Bevel Twins (Falloon)
Ducati Desmodue Twins (Falloon)
Ducati Desmoquattro Twins – 851, 888, 916, 996, 998,
   ST4 1988 to 2004 (Falloon)
Hinckley Triumph triples & fours 750, 900, 955, 1000,
   1050, 1200 – 1991-2009 (Henshaw)
Honda CBR FireBlade (Henshaw)
Honda CBR600 Hurricane (Henshaw)
Honda SOHC Fours 1969-1984 (Henshaw)
Kawasaki Z1 & Z900 (Orritt)
Moto Guzzi 2-valve big twins (Falloon)
Norton Commando (Henshaw)
Triumph 350 & 500 Twins (Henshaw)
Triumph Bonneville (Henshaw)
Triumph Thunderbird, Trophy & Tiger (Henshaw)
Velocette 350 & 500 Singles 1946 to 1970 (Henshaw)

Biographies
Chris Carter at Large – Stories from a lifetime in
   motorcycle racing (Carter & Skelton)
Jim Redman – 6 Times World Motorcycle Champion: The
   Autobiography (Redman)
'Sox' – Gary Hocking – the forgotten World Motorcycle
   Champion (Hughes)

General
BMW Boxer Twins 1970-1995 Bible, The (Falloon)
BMW Cafe Racers (Cloesen)
BMW Custom Motorcycles – Choppers, Cruisers,
   Bobbers, Trikes & Quads (Cloesen)
Bonjour – Is this Italy? (Turner)
British 250cc Racing Motorcycles (Pereira)
British Café Racers (Cloesen)
British Custom Motorcycles – The Brit Chop – choppers,
   cruisers, bobbers & trikes (Cloesen)
BSA Bantam Bible, The (Henshaw)
BSA Motorcycles – the final evolution (Jones)

Ducati 750 Bible, The (Falloon)
Ducati 750 SS 'round-case' 1974, The Book of the
   (Falloon)
Ducati 860, 900 and Mille Bible, The (Falloon)
Ducati Monster Bible (New Updated & Revised Edition),
   The (Falloon)
Ducati Story, The – 6th Edition (Falloon)
Ducati 916 (updated edition) (Falloon)
Fine Art of the Motorcycle Engine, The (Peirce)
Franklin's Indians (Sucher/Pickering/Diamond/Havelin)
From Crystal Palace to Red Square – A Hapless Biker's
   Road to Russia (Turner)
Italian Cafe Racers (Cloesen)
Italian Custom Motorcycles (Cloesen)
Kawasaki Triples Bible, The (Walker)
Kawasaki Z1 Story, The (Sheehan)
Moto Guzzi Sport & Le Mans Bible, The (Falloon)
The Moto Guzzi Story – 3rd Edition (Falloon)
Motorcycle Apprentice (Cakebread)
Motorcycle GP Racing in the 1960s (Pereira)
Motorcycle Racing with the Continental Circus
   1920-1970 (Pereira)
Motorcycle Road & Racing Chassis Designs (Noakes)
Motorcycling in the '50s (Clew)
MV Agusta Fours, The book of the classic (Falloon)
Norton Commando Bible – All models 1968 to 1978
   (Henshaw)
Off-Road Giants! (Volume 1) – Heroes of 1960s
   Motorcycle Sport (Westlake)
Off-Road Giants! (Volume 2) – Heroes of 1960s
   Motorcycle Sport (Westlake)
Off-Road Giants! (Volume 3) – Heroes of 1960s
   Motorcycle Sport (Westlake)
Racing Line – British motorcycle racing in the golden age
   of the big single (Guntrip)
The Red Baron's Ultimate Ducati Desmo Manual (Cabrera
   Choclán)
Scooter Lifestyle (Grainger)
Scooter Mania! – Recollections of the Isle of Man
   International Scooter Rally (Jackson)
Triumph Bonneville Bible (59-83) (Henshaw)
Triumph Bonneville!, Save the – The inside story of the
   Meriden Workers' Co-op (Rosamond)
Triumph Motorcycles & the Meriden Factory (Hancox)
Triumph Speed Twin & Thunderbird Bible (Woolridge)
Triumph Tiger Cub Bible (Estall)
Triumph Trophy Bible (Woolridge)
TT Talking – The TT's most exciting era – As seen by Manx
   Radio TT's lead commentator 2004-2012 (Lambert)
Velocette Motorcycles – MSS to Thruxton – Third Edition
   (Burris)
Vincent Motorcycles: The Untold Story since 1946
   (Guyony & Parker)

www.veloce.co.uk

First published in 1980 by Cassell Ltd. This reprint published in July 2018 by Veloce Publishing Limited, Veloce House, Parkway Farm Business
Park, Middle Farm Way, Poundbury, Dorchester DT1 3AR, England. Tel +44 (0)1305 260068 / Fax 01305 250479 / e-mail info@veloce.co.uk /
web www.veloce.co.uk or www.velocebooks.com.
ISBN: 978-1-787113-13-8 UPC: 6-36847-01313-4.

MIKE THE BIKE – AGAIN

THE STORY OF MIKE HAILWOOD'S RETURN TO THE TT

TED MACAULEY

FOREWORDS BY BERNIE ECCLESTONE AND JAMES TOSELAND

VELOCE PUBLISHING
THE PUBLISHER OF FINE AUTOMOTIVE BOOKS

Contents

Foreword

Ted Macauley, a long-time friend of mine, and Mike Hailwood, my motorbike race hero and Ted's best pal, took the 1978 Isle of Man TT by storm in as dramatic and romantic a comeback, against all the odds, as there could ever be. No wonder record crowds attended the spectacle that will live in their memories, and mine, for the rest of their days.

And despite the worldwide recognition and towering admiration heaped upon him at his memorable and hair-raising TT achievement on the sport's most demanding and dangerous circuit after an 11-year layoff, Mike's genuine modesty, as ever, was a tribute to the unassuming and shy genius to whom praise for his towering ability and will to win was an embarrassment.

Over my vast number of years in motorsport and Formula One, and my keen interest in motorbike racing, I have had the great pleasure of watching and getting to know a host of outstanding sportsmen, talented and brave and single-minded in their devotion to the job in hand, whatever the setbacks and dangers, and I have to say Mike was up there with the finest. And *Mike the Bike – Again* is a fitting salute to his everlasting presence in the minds of all of us who were fortunate enough to see him race – and to know him.

Bernie Ecclestone

I would like to start by saying how honoured I feel to be writing this foreword for *Mike The Bike – Again*.

When my great friend Ted Macauley called and asked me if I would like to say a few words about this incredible story, I said yes immediately.

There are no words I need to say other than "This is the most astonishing achievement any motorcyclist or sports person in any field has ever achieved."

Mike The Bike – Again is about a man so obsessed with racing motorcycles it forced him to make the bravest decision any motorcyclist has ever made.

Mike Hailwood's return to the Isle of Man TT races in 1978 was 11 years after he last took on the famous mountain course. He was 39, slightly overweight, and limped pretty badly from previous injuries he'd sustained over years of racing. These were definitely not the ideal physical stats required to wrestle a motorcycle around the 37.73-mile course at over a 100mph average.

Even with family and friends begging him not to do it, he knew it was something he had to do.

Unfortunately for me, Mike's nine world titles were all won in the 1960s before I was born. But his achievements certainly haven't faded from the

MIKE THE BIKE – AGAIN

British motorcycling fraternity. Since I was bought my first motorcycle and joined the circus of the racing paddock, Mike's name has always been godly.

With Grand Prix wins spanning over 18 years, you would have thought Mike's itch for success would have been well and truly scratched, but in 1978 it obviously came back with a vengeance.

I lived on the Isle of Man for eight years. In those eight years, I watched my friends and colleagues do something I could never have done. I was never scared of anything that involved racing a motorcycle, and when I was racing there wasn't a day that went by I didn't want to go faster on two wheels, but the TT is different.

One of the main differences for me was on the grid just before the start of the race. In my world, my engineers would grab my hand and tell me to "Wring its neck" and "Ride it like you've stolen it." On a TT grid, though, the engineers hug the rider and say, "Bring it home mate.' That's different. A difference that ingrained itself in me so much that I knew I didn't have the right discipline to ride the TT course the way it needs to be ridden. I had no problem at all with risking my life on the track if it meant having the chance to win, but when I watched the TT races for the first time I realised it was a lot easier and safer to take that mentality on to the tracks I raced on, and knew in myself I was best sticking to what I knew, as I could never change that approach.

This is why Mike's comeback for me is so incredible. He could have come back and raced at Silverstone or Brands Hatch, but that obviously wouldn't have got rid of that itch. The Isle of Man TT races will always be a rider's biggest and most dangerous challenge, and riders like Mike feel most alive the closer they are to death.

I never had the pleasure of meeting this great man, but he achieved the highest accolade anyone can achieve, and that's people's respect.

Enjoy this incredible story, and thanks again to all the motorcycle fans that appreciate what we do.

James Toseland

ABOUT THE AUTHOR

Ted Macauley is currently the Formula One reporter for the *Daily Star Sunday*, London, and weekly F1 columnist for *Gulf News*, in Dubai, UAE. He is also a regular car reviewer for five monthly magazines for Surrey Hills Publishing, and the Lifestyle Editor. He was the *Daily Mirror's* chief sports feature writer, F1 and MotoGP reporter, until his retirement from the paper in 1997.

Ted met Mike Hailwood at the Isle of Man TT in 1961 when Mike rode all four solo classes and became the first rider to win three races in a week. He was just 21. Their friendship flourished from then until Mike Hailwood's tragic death in 1981.

Ted has written three books about Mike Hailwood's life and career.

1

A spirit reborn

The TT, the world's most famous road race series, was in the doldrums until the revitalising reappearance of Mike Hailwood in 1978, and again in 1979.

It had been ravaged by the remarks of star international riders, and by boycotts, scathing criticism and, finally, by the Fédération Internationale de Motocyclismé decision to emasculate it by removing its Grand Prix status.

That august body, founded in 1904 and based in far-off Geneva, saw fit to support the condemnations heaped upon the circuit by seasoned professionals like Giacomo Agostini (15-time world champion and many times a TT winner) and Phil Read (once Agostini's MV-Agusta team-mate and another superb TT expert), and sliced the Isle of Man venue off its road race Grand Prix calendar.

Whatever the motives of the famous riders instrumental in forcing the FIM to its controversial decision, the effects soon began to bite; the TT, with its fine history of classic racing and Grand Prix combat, looked a watered-down version of what had always been a glittering occasion. In truth, it began to look doomed, even though the Manx authorities and the Auto-Cycle Union, the British organisers of home racing and the TT, the showpiece of their year, were prepared to fight tooth and nail for its survival.

The people of the Isle of Man, fearful that their prosperity might falter if their renowned race suffered many more withdrawals, were desperate to find a saviour. The ACU had done their level best, but had failed to come up with a name that could counter the loss of popularity the island was in danger of suffering. Indeed, there was only one man, one name beloved by everybody in racing, who could reverse the trend. That man was Mike Hailwood who had last competed in the TT in 1967, the year Honda, his team, announced it was quitting racing.

Mike was 38. He had suffered an horrendous Formula One Grand Prix car crash that had left one of his legs bent like a banana and his right foot locked into a flagrantly flat position with little or no movement in it. It meant he could not drive a racing car, with its need for heel-and-toe action, and be as competitive as he would like. But he could still ride a motorcycle, with the gear change switched onto the left side of the machine; and as foot braking did not come too much into play he could, taking the dust covers off his dormant talent on two wheels, probably be as competitive as anybody around. And he knew as much about the rises and dips and vagaries of the TT's 37¾-mile circuit as the island's Director of Highways.

MIKE THE BIKE – AGAIN

After his crippling crash at the Nürburgring in the 1974 German Grand Prix, Mike had moved from his home in South Africa to a new base in Auckland, New Zealand, but had become bored with life so far away from all his friends in Britain. The stirrings of his competitive instincts had reawakened the almost desperate urge to pit his skill against somebody else's once more.

There was an uncontrollable restlessness about him, a feeling of well-being and an inner knowledge and confidence that he could mix it with the best and do nothing to impair the legendary reputation he had built for himself, that made it almost essential for him to come back, and to come back where the challenge was the toughest of them all ... at the TT.

When we had sorted out the details, fixed the machinery and the support, we were able to announce the news that set the racing world back on its heels. It also caused one of the biggest upsurges in attendance at the TT for years; hoteliers rubbed their hands, cab drivers and shopkeepers and cafe owners looked on June 1978 as the year that would give them record profits. There would have been a record crowd, too, but Geoff Duke's ferry from Heysham, on the north-west Lancashire coast, to the Isle of Man's capital, Douglas, broke down and some enthusiasts could not make it. They missed a treat, a fairy tale return for the maestro with a win in his first race, the Formula One event, a world title to go with it – his tenth, and his 13th TT win.

The scenes were unforgettable; the gratitude of the Manx people was warm, and the memories for the out-and-out enthusiasts were something they would treasure down the years. Hailwood had given them a lifetime of excitement in one week.

He could not walk the street without being mobbed; he could not drink, or sit, or eat in our hotel without being approached by well-wishers. Seven television and film crews sent his name and that of the Isle of Man circling the globe. Newspapers and magazines pinpointed that speck of land in the Irish Sea, and it became known as the Isle of Mike ...

And yet, when the chairman of the Tourist Board, Mr Clifford Irving, was asked by a bubblingly excited Member of the House of Keys – the island's parliament – if the Isle of Man should officially record the Manx people's gratitude with a silver salver, he thrust his hands deep into his trouser pockets, rubbed the toe of his highly polished shoe in the grit behind the grandstand and said, after a considered pause: "No, I don't think so."

You would have thought that Mr Irving was being asked to grant Hailwood a knighthood; there was not an islander who would have refused it, had it been in his power.

One year later, in 1979, when Mike went back again, won once more and attracted an absolute record crowd of more than 50,000 for the entire week of racing, those same islanders whose commercial gatherings had faltered for the time before and after the TT, would have crowned him King of Man. But he still did not get an official salver, or clock, or plaque, or anything else that reflected the feelings of the people who had benefited so grandly from his pulling power as the greatest motorcycle racer of all time over the sport's most spectacular stage.

Young Mike learning to ski.

Mike aged about ten, ripping up the lawn of his parents' home near Oxford.

Mike enjoying skiing in Switzerland ...

... and relaxing on the slopes there.

Mike tries his hand in a racing car.

Mike and a very battered MV 500 in the 1965 Senior TT. Despite crashing, he remounted and went on to win the race.

Relaxing at home.

A wonderful collection of Mike's racing trophies.

Douglas IOM during TT week.

Mike and Ted walking in the pit lane, 1978.

Still basically a production motorcycle, the big V-twin Ducati as it is fettled for the 1978 TT.

Steve Wynn of Sports Motorcycles and
Mike on the start line, F1 TT 1978.

Dawn practice on the island – 5am on a cold June morning in 1978.
Notice the repairs to Mike's boot, scraped open by hard cornering.

2

Disguised among the amateurs

There has always been an affinity between Mike Hailwood and the TT. He has revelled in the challenge it offers, and, at the same time, respected its unforgiving nature. It has, in his opinion, always been the ultimate confrontation for the man who races motorcycles. The awful fact that more than 100 men had been killed in trying to master its many pitfalls, up until the time he made his comeback in 1978, held no fears whatever for him, even though he knew he would have to go faster than anybody else to take up his reputation where he had left off 11 years before.

Mike and I had chatted in a superficial way about the TT early in 1977, when it was obvious he was getting somewhere near to the sort of fitness and muscular robustness he had always enjoyed. It was fanciful banter; the conversation, it seemed to me, of two dreamers. Silly old buggers, in his words. But it was clear to us both that the TT was turning into a two-man show, Mick Grant versus John Williams, with little else to excite the imagination outside these two great riders.

It was a conversation which, like the drinks that went with it, soon vanished; under the surface, however (and wisdom only came with hindsight), Mike was evidently looking for some sort of support to bolster his confidence enough to tackle the TT again.

When the flap on my letter box snapped open and shut just after breakfast on the morning of 11 July 1977, there was a light blue airmail letter lying on the floor of the porch. It was postmarked Auckland, New Zealand, and it was addressed in Mike's broad handwriting.

Inside, in his usual terrible typing, was a long letter, much longer than he normally wrote. He gossiped about the TT that had just gone, a long weekend he had been on with his wife Pauline to Melbourne in Australia. There was some chatter about a first and three thirds at a vintage motorcycle meeting, and a whole wad of words about a shopping spree and what a nice, relaxed and peaceful time he was enjoying. The crunch came farther down the page.

Here's what he wrote:

And now for something completely different. How would you like to make some money? Yes! Well, so would I.

Here's how. Wait for it ... I'm thinking of having another bash at the TT next year (silly old sod, you'll say), and all the races, the little vintage and no account meetings, I've been doing have been in exploration of the idea.

I don't think it's a good idea – and I can hear you agreeing – for all the usual reasons. It's irresponsible, selfish, I'm too old, I'm physically out of shape, etc, etc, but I still have the urge and the money would come in rather handy.

I'd like to do the Formula One and, possibly, 250 and 350; I don't believe I could manage the 500 or 750. What do you think?

I would like us to keep this ultra, ULTRA secret and we must talk only to top people and swear them to secrecy. It all depends on how I feel after I've done a six-hour Production race in Sydney, Australia, on a 900cc Ducati. Then, if I feel I can be competitive and am physically capable, I would be keen to do the Isle of Man and go through with this ridiculous plan.

His one great regret was that he did not want to let his wife Pauline in on his idea. He felt it might upset her that, after such a narrow escape from death only three years before, he was prepared to return to racing motorcycles. We agreed only to 'phone or correspond through his business address, the marine engineering company he had formed with his friend, former Yardley McLaren team manager Phil Kerr, the laconic New Zealander.

Neither Mike nor I gave Pauline enough credit for astute observation. She had watched his growing keenness whenever he went racing the vintage bikes, usually in Australia, and had noted that all his old flair and style were still there.

She told me later, when we revealed to her Mike's TT plans: "I knew he would do it. I could see it building up in him, but there was no way I was going to stop him, or do anything to put him off. That might have driven him away and, plainly, the need to race was still very much in him. Anyway, he was, and still can be, the best in the world, so why should I stand in his way?

"But I can't say I'm overjoyed at the idea ..."

My reply to Mike's letter was that I had always suspected there was a vein of madness running through him – and now I was sure of it. But on the basis that he knew his own mind, and had assessed and come to terms with the risks and the problems involved in such a massive enterprise, I was happy to organise his comeback to the TT.

From the outset – and this is nothing to do with being wise after the event – I was confident he would win certainly one race, maybe two, and that he would not let anybody down, least of all himself.

There were, naturally, a few detractors who, not knowing the depth of Mike's honesty and determination to do well, looked on the announcement of his return to TT racing as some sort of publicity gimmick, (though to what end I cannot imagine) or worse, as the ill-advised attempt of a former champion to recapture some lost glory.

Advice came in thick and fast, and despite our plan to play it all low key, without boast or false bolster to our hopes, there were those who wanted publicly to put themselves into a position where they could say: 'See, I told you so ...'

One race chief, whose lack of finesse must always guarantee his anonymity, was so anxious to discount any threat that Mike might offer his men that he rushed rashly into print with the empty claim that he had turned down a request from Mike to join his team – and then listed the reasons why. That it was a fatuous figment, since no such approach had been made either by me or Mike, merely demonstrated just how quickly people without vision were prepared to discount Hailwood as a no-hoper.

After our initial anger at the man's brazen, if less than accurate, boasts we settled to enjoy the feeling of embarrassment that would flood him when Mike, as we knew he could, won a TT and he was left to explain to his superiors why, if his claims were to be believed by them, he had turned down the man who was the hub of the world-wide publicity at the races. The fact that it all came true later was more than enough reward for both of us, for it certainly muffled his trumpetings.

For every one like him there were ten others who shared our belief that any investment in Mike's comeback would pay off, but they had to be convinced he was not doing it just for the money. And this was a tricky operation; people imagined that Mike was out to grab a vast fortune for himself. It was even suggested to me that he was broke and needed the cash. Nothing, however, could have been further from the truth. His father Stan, a millionaire motorcycle dealer with the biggest chain of showrooms in the country at one time, had died and had left Mike well off. No, the plain truth was, just as he had said in his letter to me, he still had the urge to race and he loved the TT.

It was important not to frighten off people who could provide the necessary sponsorship; the mere mention of Mike's name could have them believing he was priced right out of their market. So I had to make sure that it did not happen and that word got round quickly that Hailwood was racing again for the sheer enjoyment of doing it, but not at his own cost.

Five miles from where I live in Manchester, at the far end of Deansgate near the city centre, there is a motorcycle sales business run by a bearded race enthusiast called Steve Wynne – 'Sports Motorcycles'. And in 1977 they had provided a big Ducati for Welshman Roger Nicholls that had all but won the Formula One TT.

The fact that the race went to Phil Read on a Honda was due almost entirely to the fact that in pouring rain it was cut to four laps from its original five. Nicholls had already stopped to refuel in the gathering gloom but Read, just behind him, was waved to go straight through without a stop by his pit helpers and he was able to put enough distance between him and the desperate Nicholls to clinch the race. I never forgot it; morally, it seemed to me, Nicholls had won but the ill-timed release of the news by the officials that the race had been cut worked for Read and against Nicholls.

So when it came to planning Mike's Formula One ride I turned to Steve Wynne and his partner, John Sear, at Sports Motorcycles. The Ducati was obviously a potential winner – but I wanted more. Honda, with their vast resources, would have spent the year improving on their Formula One machine; Ducati, on the other hand, were content with the status quo.

I needed an escape clause, if you like, in case Mike failed in the Formula One race, the first of the week and therefore the most important. It had to be seen that if the Ducati was beaten by the Honda it was only because of the latter's superior speed and advanced stage of development – and that it was no fault of Mike's. And, on the face of it, it seemed to be certain that there was no way the Honda, ridden by Read again, could be beaten by the Italian machine. Mike had to start as the underdog, and anything more than just a finish in his first race over the circuit for eleven years just had to be a bonus. In fact, the Honda was faster and did handle better than the Ducati: and the Ducati was being provided by a small North of England company, while the Honda had the might of the famous factory behind it.

It was important, too, to let the racing world know that Mike had signed for Steve Wynne's little-known company, because it was pretty obvious that they could not afford to be paying the ransom that everybody thought he must be asking. But it was also important not to lose sight of the fact that, with Mike aboard, the Ducati just had to be a dark horse, one that was in with a very good chance of winning even if we did not make that boast a clarion call to start the rest trembling.

Steve, John and Pat Slinn, who was later to join the company, and I all went to dinner to clinch the deal. When I told them how much we wanted they all put their knives and forks down with a clatter, mouths dropped open to be replaced with wide grins when I repeated the figure. It was not much more than the price of the dinner – and I do not eat a lot. They, like everybody else, had expected to be hammered with an unreasonable demand, the price of buying a legend, and were grouping to haggle furiously. Their relief was evident; I am not sure they did not suspect I was somebody masquerading as me and leading them into a cruel knock-back.

The details were quickly sorted out and my purposes were served. For in quick order Sports Motorcycles had spread the word, officially and unofficially throughout the business, that they had landed the bargain of a lifetime in signing Mike to ride the Ducati and lead their team at the TT. Their excitement knew no limits, and even if they did not release the precise figure they made certain everybody knew they had secured the skill of the greatest rider of all time at a bargain they could hardly believe.

Yamaha were next. Two old friends, Rodney Gould, a former 250cc World Champion, and Paul Butler, who had both worked for the company in Amstelveen on the outskirts of Amsterdam, could scarcely contain their excitement when I made the initial approaches. They both worked tremendously hard to convince their Japanese bosses that the publicity haul from such a venture would be immense – though there was a detectable reluctance from the hierarchy.

Mike flew home from New Zealand while Yamaha pondered the possibilities. We went to the British Grand Prix at Silverstone and, after watching Giacomo Agostini flounder embarrassingly in twelfth place on the works 500cc Yamaha, had a meeting behind locked doors with TT supremo Vernon Cooper, an unashamed admirer of Mike as a man and as a rider, and when I put it to him that we had plans for the famous Isle of Man race the following year, 1978, we agreed a price and settled the whole deal in a little over ten minutes. Such was Cooper's enthusiasm – shrewd man that he is, he had recognised the unpalatable truth that the TT was gasping for air, and the appearance of Hailwood would be pure oxygen.

I stressed to him that Mike was not entering the TT to play about: it was to be a serious confrontation with the circuit he had challenged so often and so spectacularly before, and whilst Mike was not going to kill himself in the effort to entertain he was fully prepared to give value for money. If Cooper had any doubts at all they were dashed by Mike's firmness of expression, his totally transparent honesty, and the self-effacement, with which he delivered his short, but telling, homily on his plans for his comeback.

Vernon Cooper, most times an oasis of good sense in what is a positive desert of barren thought on the way racing should be run, brings an astute business brain into play when he can see that benefits will accrue from firm decisions. And when the issue of Mike's reappearance at the TT came within his orbit, and after he had met the great man face-to-face, he quickly assessed the magnitude of the returns against the outlay, and found very much in favour of the plan. His only concern was for Mike's safety: an essential factor. Nobody wanted to be the prime mover in a comeback for Mike that ended in disaster. But Mike himself offered reassurances that dispelled any doubts about that possibility.

The subtlety of Mike's thinking was that he could adequately cope with whatever the TT threw at him in terms of competition or difficulty of circuit, and still not have to stretch himself to more than 80 per cent of his ability. This was not an assessment based on conceit, but purely a cold, clinical look at his own skills honestly compared with those of the other riders likely to be entered in the races he would contest. I am certain that Cooper, who had never met Mike before, recognised this rather chilling sureness in his make-up, even though it was never mentioned. He walked back into the Silverstone sunshine from the secrecy and shade of the office under the administration block, happy in the knowledge that he had just agreed to back the most unique twist of fate in the history of the TT.

MIKE THE BIKE – AGAIN

It was still to be a cloak and dagger operation, for the deal with Yamaha was still to be swung and there was Mike's October date with the six-hour race in Sydney, the final fitness hurdle that would prove to him that he was in good enough shape to withstand the gruelling rigours of the TT course.

There was not much doubt that Yamaha would come through with the machines we wanted, and Steve Wynne was well under way with sorting out the Ducati Supersport for the Formula One class. It was now just a matter of time and filling in the gap between announcement and participation in the most useful, viable way possible. That meant another look at the TT course.

That is where the Manx Grand Prix came in useful; it is a race for amateurs over the TT course and held in the first week of every September. I arranged with the Clerk of the Course, a former TT rider, Jackie Wood, that we could slip Mike in among the practising riders as anonymously as possible on the pretext of his doing some filming. Indeed, he did have a camera set up on a machine and helped with some footage for a pseudo-American movie-maker who promised Mike a fee and insurance cover of £125, and came up with neither.

The most vital factor was that Mike was able, through the infinite kindness and understanding of the MGP organisers, to get in some vital laps in his September reprise of his earlier records.

A famous race family, the Padgetts, as Yorkshire as they come but based in Douglas in the Isle of Man, offered to lend Mike two bikes for a try-out. So we went to Jurby, an old Royal Air Force air strip on the north-west of the island, though with its gravelled main straight and moving surface it was maybe not the best of places for a test run. But it was the only one, really, before Mike could be turned loose among the Manx Grand Prix hopefuls.

Right from the off, when the beefy looking OW31 750cc Yamaha was unloaded from the Padgett's van, Mike was invaded with doubt and apprehension. He did not like the look of it and stood distanced from it for a moment or two, eyeing it warily like a man who expected it to roar into life by itself and bite him. And when Peter Padgett, the family sage, finally persuaded him to give it a shove he struggled for ages to get it started, filling the air with frustrated curses. It was certainly not love at first sight.

When it eventually fired up, and that terrifying 120 brake horsepower bit into its power band, Mike was whirled up the straight in a blur, faster even than he believed the thing would be. But he persevered and after two or three bursts finally got his head down.

'He's enjoying it now,' said Peter Padgett, smiling with relief, 'he's really going good on it. And he LOOKS good on it, too. The lad's having a grand old time now. Just look at him – he's lost nowt of his old flair. And there's no way he's going to let that bugger beat him.'

The wind was whistling across che flats of the airfield when Mike wheeled the big OW3 I in a wide circle to head back to the spot from which we are all watching.

'No, thank you. Thanks, but no thanks, there's no way I'm gonna ride that bloody thing in any race,' said Mike as Peter's mouth sagged open. 'It's like a bloody aeroplane. No wonder you brought me up here to test it, more fitting than on a track. And you tell me the thing's out of fettle! I'd be mad to stick myself in against the likes of Mick Grant and John Williams on that thing.' He stepped back from it as if it was going to explode at any second ...

'You can put it back in the van,' he said, 'let me have a go on the 350 – I'll be able to handle that.'

Peter argued the merits of the 750, its smoothness of power and its marvellous handling characteristics against the sheer hard labour of riding the smaller machine.

But Mike insisted the 750 was out, definitely, and the 350, once he had tested it, was in. He flew up the straight, put it into a big arc to come back, and squealed the bike to a halt in front of the van. 'Talk about hard work,' he smiled, 'you're right, Pete, it looks as if it's the other one for me.' And that was that. But in the car going back along the TT course to our hotel in Douglas, Mike was still not convinced in his own mind that he was doing the right thing in agreeing to ride the 750, whether it was in among the amateurs practising for the MGP, or the hurly-burly of the TT, the world's toughest race.

'I must be mad, but I'll have to put in some really hard laps anywhere I can to get used to that thing,' he said. 'It's a rocket ship, and no doubt it will be a handful of problems. Maybe I should just enter the 500cc race and leave it at that; I just do not like the big fella. There's too much power for anybody's good and it certainly does not fill me with confidence. And, remember, I was only riding it in straight lines. I'll have to have a good think about that one ...'

He was as nervous as a newcomer when he joined the long queue of starters, all absolute strangers, for the Manx Grand Prix practice session. Perhaps too much fuss, which there was, had made him edgy, or it may have been that even at that distance from the TT, still nearly ten months off, he had begun to feel the pressure.

The Padgeus had done a good job in trying to keep him calm and unruffled, but he still did not like the 750 even though they, knowing his reputation as a man who could ride any machine, thought he was joking with them.

We had disguised him as best we could in borrowed red leathers that owed rather more to Mr Michelin than to any sleekness of design, and a blue helmet, livery far removed in colour and style from that associated with him. But we did not want any of the ambitious and eager young scalp hunters of the MOP recognising him and trying to make a race of it, either for their sake or ours.

Forty or so men pushed off under the timekeepers' gaze in the grandstand area of the famous TT course overlooking the isle's capital, Douglas, and the grey Irish Sea in the far distance.

MIKE THE BIKE – AGAIN

Then Mike went, the big 750 superbike resting heavily against his right hip until he manhandled it off the line and fired it into life. Only then did all the awkwardness and ungainliness he showed in walking on that bent right leg evaporate. He was transformed into the superbly balanced athlete he had always been, comfortable on the machine, like part of it, arms at full stretch, eyes crystal and all-seeing, crouched behind the fairing like a man who was hell bent on a record opening lap in the most important ride of his life. And, in a way, it was.

In the motley dash and gamble on lines that the official Grand Prix field demonstrated, it was easy to pick out Mike, belting furiously down Bray Hill, riding the suspension-testing bounce at the bottom, and sloping majestically into and out of Quarter Bridge, heading for the wriggles and twists and pitfalls of the country roads and mountain highs.

He was back 72 minutes later: a lot of men had been overtaken and had wondered who on earth the rider could have been who left them trailing in his slipstream.

He was content to give the Yamaha three bursts; after that 15-minute test session at Jurby he had not been confident enough to do more. But those three, near flat-out dashes left him with enough respect for the sheer brute force of the machine to take no silly risks on it.

He stopped three times to change film, signed autographs at every halt and tried hard to concentrate on the commentary he was making into a microphone taped onto his helmet. Then, in one of his 165-mile-an-hour bursts, his leathers peeled open to the waist and he stopped again to do them up. When we had estimated all the halts we worked out he had done a lap equal to about 25 minutes ... I was happy that despite all those attacks on his concentration he had covered the circuit on his fact-finding mission in a respectable time.

His first reaction when we got back to the hotel was one utterly different from what I expected. He said: 'It's staggering how people have remembered me after all these years. Quite fantastic. And everywhere I stopped people kept asking me for my autograph, or they wanted to take a picture. I can hardly believe it.'

Nothing, until I pressed him, about how the lap went. His astounding self-effacement was such that he was utterly overcome by the response of the crowd and the riders in the MGP, all of whom stared unashamedly or tried to get close enough to their idol to snatch a personal word with him.

The 750 had done nothing, really, to endear itself. Mike's feelings about it wavered between terror and mild doubt because of its awesome power, though he agreed that its ability to soak up the TT course's bumps in its monoshock suspension system was a boon.

'The OW31 really is terrifyingly fast,' he said, 'quicker than anything I've ever ridden. It's a far greater kick than a Formula One car. Honestly, and I know people think I'm joking, it scared the life out of me. I gave it two or three full-out bursts on the smoother bits of road and it nearly threw me off the back. I felt as if my arms were coming away from my shoulders, there's so much pull. It's bloody fearsome, but I suppose I'll get used to it. I won't like it, but I'll get used to it.'

The belly pan of the Yamaha was found to be severely scraped, the footrests almost sharpened, and the expansion chamber flattened. 'I don't remember doing all that,' he said, genuinely puzzled, 'but I did feel a big bang at one stage and I thought I may have bottomed it.' The holes in his boots after one lap – and a slow one at that – looked like most other men's after two or three races.

Over dinner in our beachside hotel Mike told me: 'It was really good to be back on the TT course, though I'd forgotten a lot of it. Ten years is a long time to be away from a place and at racing speeds you don't get too much time to reset your memory banks when you're coming up to a corner. The TT is one place where you have to be dead certain or you are a goner.

'There's no room for guesswork here. And, obviously, I'm going to have to put in lots more laps before I can even try to be competitive. I'm going to come to the island three weeks before the race and get some time in on a bike and in a car.

'I really enjoyed myself tonight – when I wasn't shaking with fear on that 750. I'd had only quarter of an hour to try to come to terms with it and to get some idea of what it might do, and all that in a straight line at Jurby, the old airfield, but when I got out there tonight and let it go it made my eyes water. It's the quickest thing I've ever ridden.

'The course has been improved very much since I last raced here in 1967, but that 750 showed me corners that aren't there with any other machine. Some of the bad surface that I remember has been smoothed but, again, on the big Yamaha some of the old bumps seem even bigger.

'What with doing the commentary, changing batteries and film cassettes, stopping here, there and everywhere, and having to read a complicated list of instructions on how to work the camera, I had plenty to worry about. Trying to keep the bike in a straight line at a decent speed didn't help.

'The lads who have been racing them have all my sympathy and admiration – they have earned their money. I just don't know how they stay on them and I don't feel brave enough to try.'

Within a few months, on a Yamaha 750-four borrowed from Bob Haldane, he was only 1.5 seconds outside Grand Prix regular Gregg Hansford's outright lap record set on the works Kawasaki at Pukehoe, New Zealand ... and he was only testing.

The bandwagon begins to roll

Phil Read, winner of the 1977 Formula One TT and, obviously, Mike's sternest rival for the laurels in 1978, sent his old Grand Prix adversary a telegram when he heard the news about the comeback.

It said: 'Looking forward to seeing you in the island – behind me, of course.'

Mike's reply went: 'Only when I'm lapping you ... ' And it seemed pretty evident that he was starting to enjoy the build-up to the TT; sure, there was plenty of ballyhoo but I believe he half expected it, though the sheer intensity of it probably took him by surprise.

It was all accelerated when Martini, the world famous drinks firm, came on the scene. They were really the final touch of glamour on what was turning into an extremely glossy occasion.

For sheer style they were unbeatable, their name was international, their support magnificent and, even if they were at times a little too fussy, they coloured the entire venture with a finesse that could not have been matched by anybody else.

Yamaha, ever mindful of the need to grab whatever headlines they could, had recognised that Mike's return to the TT was a publicity opportunity that was far too good to miss. After the briefest intervals between the time I approached them for machines and their agreement to supply them we were promised whatever we needed – but they would not pay Mike any money at all to race their marque.

Just before Christmas, 1977, with Martini already in as principal sponsors, I had a letter from Yamaha, Amsterdam, confirming their support, too. There had been much high-ranking discussion behind the scenes at Yamaha in Japan followed by telexes and 'phone calls to Amsterdam urging help for Team Martini-Hailwood ...

The letter said:

Further to your letter ... on the appearance of Mike Hailwood in the 1978 Isle of Man TT races, I am glad to confirm to you the following arrangements:

Yamaha Motor NV will be happy to loan Mike with either a TZ250 or TZ350, a TZ750 and a 500cc four-cylinder Grand Prix machine as used by Giacomo Agostini during the 1977 season.

There are certain things, however, that must be stressed. Firstly, this arrangement covers only the 1978 Isle of Man TT races. Should Mike wish to contest any other races during the season, we can at least discuss the possibility of the loan of a TZ350 or 250 and a TZ750, but under no circumstances can we provide the 500cc GP machine for any event other than the Isle of Man TT.

Secondly, while we are happy to assist with machinery we cannot make any actual financial contribution to Mike's effort.

We are glad to hear that Martini-Rossi will be sponsoring the Isle of Man effort. Like ourselves, they are one of the most respected names in their particular sphere of business and we are sure that the association will be to our mutual benefit.

It was ironic that the Agostini 500 was the one Mike and I had watched at Silverstone only five months before – and we had both squirmed seeing the once great Italian, on the best works machinery, being humiliated by men of much less skill than his. Though we both felt the bike was a potential winner at the TT.

I recruited Mike's former mechanic, Nobby Clarke, once with Honda, now looking after Kenny Roberts at Yamaha, Trevor Tilbury, the Yamaha 250cc specialist, and Jerry Wood, an old friend of Mike's and the workshop manager at Yamaha, Amsterdam. We agreed to pay their wages and hotel bills – Yamaha agreed to free them for the TT fortnight of racing and practice.

Mike was delighted that Nobby, in whom he had a lot of faith, could join the team. Jerry, too, was a great boost to morale, he felt, though he did not know Tilbury.

Robert Jackson at Mitsui, the Yamaha distributors in the United Kingdom, was appointed link man between the factory and the team and liaised with Martini in the promotional side of the effort.

Mike returned from Auckland to be a guest on the *This is Your Life* TV show featuring Barry Sheene, the young World Champion. If anybody had any doubts about Mike's seriousness they were soon dispelled. He was tanned and fit, he had none of the belly that had girdled him in September, his double chin had gone and so had 14lb in spare weight – the result of a campaign of running, swimming and exercising.

Yamaha had promised to send him a 250 to New Zealand – but it never turned up. So he had been belting around the circuits near his home on a variety of borrowed bikes. He felt that Yamaha, by not sending him the machine he wanted, were not taking him seriously enough, and even though I pressured them, too, the bike just never got to him. But it had not put any sort of a stutter in his efforts, and he looked a picture of health, better than I had seen him for a long time.

He did not make an issue of the non-appearance of the Yamaha, but it was clear to me that he felt disappointment. Its arrival could only have been mutually beneficial, as subsequent events proved, because he never really got to grips with the lightweight machine at the TT.

MIKE THE BIKE – AGAIN

Martini cashed in on Mike's return home for the television show and organised a press conference in their penthouse suite high above the Haymarket, London. It was here, I suppose, that we felt the full impact and saw all the implications of his comeback. Three television crews were there as the centrepieces of a massive media attendance – and, as things are measured by television interest these days, it was easy to see that Mike's return was considered to be of wide interest. The Martini men could not have been happier, either with the exposure or with the man they had at the middle of it all. Mike was a model of calm through it all; he was witty, he was patient, he was, as you would always expect from him, modest and reluctant to further his own ends.

The marriage of Mike to Martini was the perfect association – they were happy with each other. And, really, it had been no gamble at all on either side.

It came to fruition after I had been to Le Mans for the Bol d'Or, the previous September. I had recognised the possibilities of a tie-up: Mike, by his reputation, his manner, his background and his box office appeal, was the sort of central figure a company like Martini could exploit. He was as upmarket as it was, but his appeal went even wider, and Martini, to its everlasting credit, was quick to recognise it.

I had been a guest in the Martini all-night restaurant at Le Mans and had mentioned my ideas to its Paris-based sales and promotion men, and they in turn referred me to their London office. We arranged a meeting in Manchester, my home city, and a dapper, deep-voiced Tony Beardmore came to see me.

Normally, I don't suppose a famous cocktail company like Martini would have been remotely interested in any sort of connection with motorcycle racing – its image is nearer ale than aperitifs. But because Mike was to be the central promotional figure, Martini's interest was quickly fuelled.

Beardmore had done his homework. He knew Mike's pedigree: he knew all about his MBE, his George Medal for bravery in rescuing a fellow Grand Prix racing driver from a blazing car, his record in world championships, and his further potential from their point of view. It was almost an action replay of the deal done with Vernon Cooper, the ACU road race chief at Silverstone: it was all over quite quickly. A sum was agreed, a plan of campaign mapped out and the returns fully anticipated to our mutual satisfaction. The full weight of Martini then fell in behind us, the promotional jackets (though I was not included when they budgeted for them), caps, T-shirts, overalls and motifs ...

When we took the lift up to the penthouse of the Martini Terrace in London for the press conference, Mike was in a borrowed suit, a pair of shoes that were a size too small – taken from a friend's wardrobe – my shirt, somebody else's tie, but his own socks. It was 10am on 17 January 1978.

Just the night before he had heard that his father, Stan Hailwood, had collapsed on a beach in Miami, had been in and out of a nearby hospital and had flown to Barbados where he was desperately ill. Mike's concentration on the press conference and his rapt attention to people who wanted to talk to him (and there were many), was a masterpiece of unstinting effort; with Stan so ill and wanting to see him Mike's mind must have been in a turmoil. But you would never have detected it.

At a private meeting before the conference got under way he had said: 'I just hope I don't let you all down. I'm not daft enough to think I can win, but I'm daft enough to try. And I will.'

I told him that everybody else concerned with the enterprise had already won: Martini ... Yamaha ... Dunlop ... Castrol ... and the only pressure on him was from himself.

At the conference he flitted among the crowds of media men, did three television interviews, a live talk-in radio broadcast and then told the gathering: 'Please don't expect too much from me. This all started as a bit of fun, I suppose I must have been naive to believe it could have stayed that way. But I realise a lot of people have put a lot of money behind the scheme and I shall be doing my very best not to let anybody down.'

He met Steve Wynne from Sports Motorcycles for the first time in his life – the man who was gambling £7,000 of his own money on the Ducati in a bid to see his hero come first in the TT. They hit it off right away. Nobby Clarke, too, flew in from Holland just to have a drink with the rider he idolised and to promise: 'I've got a few good bits for the bikes hidden away in Amsterdam – and a bloody good 750 engine for you.'

That was one promise Mike did not relish, and it brought the reply: 'Well, you'd better drop it in one of the canals. I'm scared enough on the bad engines ... '

Within two days I was going to Dakar in Senegal, West Africa, on a Yamaha test trip and Mike was invited to come along. Instead, he had to fly out to the West Indies to see Stan, who was by then dying.

'It doesn't look like the old man will be able to see me race in the TT,' he said, 'and that'll really upset him. I'd love him to have been there. But it's no go.'

Mike spent five hours on the ground, sitting in a fog-shrouded jet at Heathrow, until he was told the flight was being postponed until a day later. When he got to Barbados he set up in a hotel near the hospital. Though Stan wanted to leave and return to the South of France, a region he really loved and knew well, he died early in March 1978, a month before Mike's birthday.

Mike flew on to New Zealand and got down to the grind of getting fitter: he persevered with Bob Haldane's 750 and another friend's 350 in the absence of any machinery from Yamaha, and logged about 170 laps on a circuit near Auckland.

'And I didn't have one "moment" in all the time I was testing,' he told me on the 'phone, 'not one. It all went good. Just right on plan. In fact the only scare I've had is the one with the Formula-V car. And then ... '

'What scare with what Formula-V car?' I almost yelled down the 'phone.

'Oh, I forgot to tell you,' his reply crackled back. 'I got sideswiped. And it did my old heart no good at all.

'I was testing, minding my own business as usual, when this guy came hurtling by in this big F-Y motor. Well, he lost it in a big way when he was up alongside me. He couldn't get the thing under control again and it slammed into me. I stayed on okay, but I don't know how, more by luck than judgement, that's for sure. I got into a great big wobble, and I wasn't hanging about, but I got it down to about 60 miles an hour and straightened it up.

'He bloody well banged my leg into the chain. It hurt a bit, but it's okay now. There doesn't seem to be any damage done. The only trouble was that I couldn't stop shaking for about ten minutes. I was like a jelly.'

In the light of a rather testy telephone conversation I had gone through with Martini's Tony Beardmore, this news of Mike's did not help my nerves at all.

Beardmore had taken what I thought was violent exception to a move we had made to have Mike do a demonstration lap at Donington Park, near Derby in the north Midlands, to help out his old friend Peter Gaydon, the managing director.

It was the usual style-a lap, a wave of the hand to the crowd. Nothing more than that. But Beardmore felt it was too dangerous a venture and wanted it stopped.

When I challenged him and told him precisely what the demonstration lap amounted to-a few weeks before the TT-he sounded off quite vehemently that it would only take a freak gust of wind while Mike was riding one-handed to blow him off his machine. My feeling was that the only gust of wind was coming from Martini ...

The motives supporting Beardmore's protest were, I suppose, justified in his own mind, but I felt he had failed to grasp the realities of the issue. Mike's sense of responsibility, I said, was enough protection of everybody's interests. But Beardmore would not hear of it and insisted, despite my protests that if he watched Mike in serious practice he might have a coronary, that the whole thing should be called off until after the TT.

I just dared not tell him that Mike had been swiped sideways by a racing car. What that would have done to him I cannot imagine, since he was having the vapours at the thought of Mike riding, sometimes one-handed while he waved the other, on a circuit devoid of any other traffic.

The telephone lines became hot between him and me – and then between him and Amsterdam, Yamaha's headquarters. Then, naturally, from Amsterdam to me. It was an impossibly silly situation and I called Mike to tell Beardmore so; his reply cannot be written here.

Nobody could fault Beardmore's integrity – and in many ways it was admirable – but I thought it showed excessive anxiety.

The letter he wrote – something of a rebuke in its own way, and I must say I felt as if I had been reprimanded – went:

Further to our various telephone conversations of today, there are a number of points which I feel I should now confirm in writing. The first of these concerns the appearance of Mike Hailwood at Donnington [sic] on 14th May, 1978. Although I have the greatest possible respect for the ability of Mike, especially when mounted on two wheels, I must reiterate the view that I still consider there is a distinct element of risk in Mike riding on a circuit so shortly before he is contracted to appear at the Isle of Man.

Mishaps can regretfully happen to even the world's greatest and far be it from me to wish it upon him, but were something untoward to happen and Mike should fall awkwardly, especially since he would probably have only one hand on the handlebars, whilst waving to the crowd with the other, this could put him out of the Isle of Man ...

Whatever criticisms are levelled at the often autocratic big money sponsors, and there are plenty, the Martini involvement and the superbly professional way in which they operated left no room for carping – nor for the sort of embarrassment less sensitive companies cause their stars.

I will never forget the telex message sent by Fabergé, the perfume people, to their man Barry Sheene, bidding to beat Kenny Roberts at the Nürburgring, West Germany, in 1978. Hilarious sincerity shone from misplaced commercialism. The telex read: 'When you get in the "Ring" ride like hell, beat Kenny Roberts with your great smell.'

It was a communication which understandably enjoyed only restricted circulation.

It was just about this time I had a phone call from Mick Grant, the fastest man ever at the TT with 191mph recorded on the radar trap, offering to help Mike all he could.

Mick, a miner's son from Yorkshire, is one of the great riders of the Isle of Man circuit and as well renowned for his blunt, no-nonsense approach as he is for his bravery on road circuits.

He said: 'Hailwood must be mad to be going back to the TT but tell him I'll help him all I can. If there's anything I can do, I will. No messing. He's been my idol since I first started racing and the idea of being up against him on the island gives me a big kick.

'He's a legend all right, but I think he might damage his image if he's not careful. There have been a lot of changes at the TT, the bikes are very much quicker, and nobody wants him to do anything daft. I'm looking forward to meeting him and having a good natter about the race.'

That lovely man John Williams, who died of heart trouble after a crash in Ireland in 1978, came to dinner at my house and said Honda must be really worried about Mike's return, because they had signed him – Williams – for the Formula One race.

John, who had been driving a canker in the winter months of 1978 to get away from the pressures of racing for a while, was, along with Grant, joint favourite to pick up the big prizes at the TT.

'But I've a feeling Mike might alter all that,' he said, 'because I don't believe, like so many others, that he's gone at the game and he's in it only for the money he can wring out of the organisers. That's rubbish; you see. He'll be one of the men to beat okay. No trouble. He'll give us all a lot of bother and I know Honda are worried about him, whatever they might say.'

John, who had met Mike a month earlier at the Motorcycle Show and had been almost shy in his presence, knew exactly what he was saying, and the wisdom of it all came true – but then there is an honesty among these men that rarely shows itself in other sports.

While Martini planned their canapé and marquee attack on the TT, and Schweppes, sponsors of the Classic race, wondered why they had feared to tread, despite my early offer to them, where Martini-Rossi had boldly gone, Mike packed his bags once again for the Isle of Man ...

... But first there was some work to be done in England. Some testing. Some psyching. And some listening, too.

To people like Steve Parrish, Barry Sheene's Suzuki teammate, who said: 'Mike Hailwood was one of the greatest riders of all time. I know that without ever having seen him race and I admire him and wish him all the best.

'But if he finishes any higher than fifth in any of the races, against the current lot of TT riders, I'll be very surprised.'

Or Irishman Tommy Robb, who used to race against Mike. He said: 'He'll go well, I've no doubt. And I fancy him to take the Formula One race on the Ducati.'

Disaster in the 1978 Senior TT race. Parliament Square, Ramsey. Dickie Attwood looks on before letting the team know back in the pits.

1978 Senior TT race. The American Pat Hennen on lap four. Shortly after, his race ended in a 165mph crash that left him in a coma for three months and ended his racing career.

Charles (Chas) Mortimer, winner of the Junior TT 1978, with Charlie Williams and Tom Herron.

Nobby Clarke, Yamaha's senior mechanic, working on Mike's bike.

Mick Grant breaks down at Ballaugh Bridge, IOM.

Mike Hailwood races on at Ballaugh Bridge, IOM.

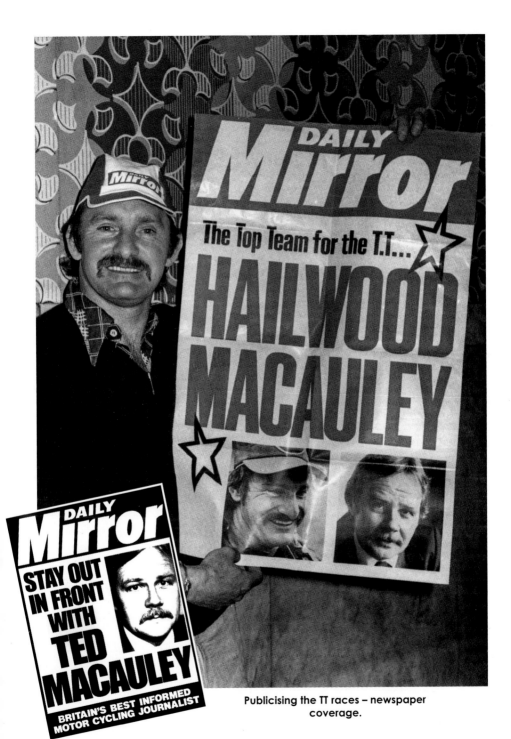

Publicising the TT races – newspaper coverage.

The Yamaha team of mechanics.

Mike Hailwood entering Parliament Square, Ramsey, IOM.

Phil Read at Quarter Bridge, Douglas, IOM.

Ted Macauley awaits news on Mike's progress during the race.

Ted Macauley dashes to see Mike after the race.

Alex George after the race.

After the F1 race, Mike with business partner Rod Gould and Phil Read.

Mick Grant, 1979 Senior TT, riding with a broken pelvis.

Ted receiving the 1978 ACU Journalist of the Year award.

Mike at a *Mike the Bike – Again* book signing in Manchester.

Mike Hailwood, Ted Macauley and Group Captain John 'Cat's Eyes' Cunningham, the famous wartime flying ace, at a presentation of the Segrave Trophy to Mike for his 1978 and 1979 TT exploits.

Mike on his Ducati at a book signing in Manchester.

Mike with a friend in Manchester.

Mike and Ted with Paul Butler and Nobby Clarke, from Yamaha, in the pit lane at Daytona, United States of America. Several weeks later, tragically, Mike was killed.

Ted with one of Mike's TT winners replicas; a treasured possession.

With the famous white, red and gold helmet on top, Mike's coffin is borne by six pall bearers, amongst them Geoff Duke (left) Dickie Attwood and James Hunt.

Memorial plaque near the TT Grandstand at the famous start line.

4

The hard way back

When Mike returned to England for his final build-up to the TT he brought with him his wife, Pauline, and their two children, David and Michelle, but they were to stay with friends near London while he tackled the job in hand.

He explained: 'It would be lovely to have them all with me in the Isle of Man, but I have enough to think about without having to worry about the family.

'It's better this way, I can concentrate fully on what I have to do. Pauline understands, she's been around racing long enough to know what I mean.'

In fact, he saw little of her through the rest of April 1978, the month he arrived from Auckland, until after the TT in June; he had his work cut out testing bikes and tyres and making appearances all over the country. It was a gruelling time for him but he took it all in his stride; pressure, after all, had been his shadow for much of his life and he was responding superbly to the new responsibilities being anchored to his shoulders.

The machines followed him – the 190mph OW31 (said to produce 120bhp but patently giving much more, though the final figure was a secret) came, and so did the big and beautiful Ducati, a thoroughbred if ever I saw one. Though there was a scare. An interpretation of the FIM rules caused a mix-up over the legality of the machine. In one text – French – it was perfectly all right, but under the English translation of the regulations for the homologation of the bike, it was not.

There had to be some frantic last-minute activity from Steve Wynne and his team to get it all sorted out, but in the end the FIM regularised the interpretation and the Ducati was declared legal.

It was a standard 900cc Supersport, the sort you could buy in any showroom, but it was stripped and painstakingly rebuilt by Wynne with weight shedding done at every stage they could. They slimmed it down to a mere 358lb, with brake horsepower rated at 85 and a speed of 175 miles an hour. Everything that could be drilled to save weight was colandered until the machine could be handled almost like a 250. It might have been a comparative lightweight but it certainly packed a punch.

I fixed test sessions and, except for Oulton Park where the director, Rex Foster, was reluctant to let us have the circuit unless Mike promised to race at one of his later meetings, everything went smoothly. Even that small problem was settled by the more sensible Chris Lowe, the organiser of racing for Motor Circuit Developments, and we were able to use the Cheshire track, so vital because so many of its features resembled the problems thrown up by the Isle of Man's bumpy circuit.

But if everything was going reasonably well for us it was not the same for John Williams and Mick Grant; they both had spills that, at one stage, put the TT in doubt for them.

John was catapulted through the screen of his bike at Imola. He found himself sitting dazedly in the middle of the tarmac at Imola, facing the wrong way and thinking the traffic had all gone around the bend. When he looked back over his shoulder he was horrified to see a bunch of riders hurtling towards him and he was bowled over. His ribs, back and kidneys were injured and he was rushed to hospital. A less than considerate doctor, not knowing, or bothering to find out, that John's ribs were cracked put him in agony when he hoisted him up in bed. John, normally the mildest of men, reacted with a reflex punch to the doctor's jaw – and then, later, discharged himself and made for home.

Then it was Mick's turn to take a tumble and he damaged a hand and later a leg, in three crashes. He was struggling, too, to regain his brilliant form. Both Honda, John's team with Phil Read, and Kawasaki, Grant's, were feeling the pinch. And all the time Mike's test sessions went smoothly – except for the rain, that is.

It splashed out of the heavens at Oulton Park, the circuit in the plush Cheshire greenery a few miles from Chester, as Mike discovered new angles to his resumed racing career.

He was jet-lagged from his trip home, the rain and the cold seeped and stabbed through his waterproofs and he was shivering and unhappy – unhappy, as much as anything, at having to put in some hard-going laps on a treacherous surface on machines that were, as yet, unfamiliar to him.

'And look at these leathers,' he said, 'they hang down between my legs. Plenty of room for a nappie – and I'll bloody well need it before this job's done.' The two Ducatis, delivered by the Bologna-based factory only the day before, stood sleekly in the pit lane. There was a gaggle of the curious and the vital around them; a workman or two from the circuit maintenance department, an engineer, a mechanic, a tyre expert, Steve Wynne, and a suspension man from Girling. It was 8am – the last thing Mike wanted to do was ride those machines, but he knew it had to be.

When they were fired up, when that deep-throated roar sent the birds flying scared from their tree perches and the tacho needle flickered up and down the dial like a metronome as Wynne twisted the throttle back and forth, Mike's smile widened and he said: 'Let's get on with it.'

The water cascaded up from the rear tyre and we could hear the gear changes almost all the way around the circuit, even though we could not see him leaning the Ducati into and out of the swoops and bends of Oulton.

He came by the pits, half crouched, going quickly in the pelting rain, but gingerly through the long curve at the bottom of the straight – and then he was once more out of sight, though not out of hearing, and a dozen men craned their necks out of anoraks and strained their ears for the crisp echo of the motor.

When he pulled in, his face under the rain dappled visor was alight with enthusiasm. The knot of those concerned grew tighter around the machine and listened eagerly to Mike's carefully weighed words and balanced opinion on what was right and what was not. And there was not much that was not.

Dunlop had produced a brand new rain tyre and the conditions had been a mixed, if miserable, blessing. After ten laps we called a halt, but it was enough for him to have found his confidence in the tyres at a peak ...

Over sandwiches and glasses of orange juice – he drank nothing stronger until after the TT – Mike told the Dunlop team: 'Those tyres are out of this world. I was so impressed. I kept leaning over and then over a bit more – and then a little bit extra. And all the time I was waiting for it to start slipping and sliding, but nothing happened. So I leaned it some more until I was far beyond the point where in the old days I'd have been down the road on my arse. But there I was ... safe ... still on board ... and thinking I could have got it over even more. More than anything this is the greatest step forward. I've seen races, of course, and I have seen guys getting the bikes well over but I didn't realise just how far you can really go, and in the rain, too. Really fantastic!

'The advances Dunlop have made in tyre technology since I last rode seriously and competitively are truly immense. I'd have never believed it, but this morning has been an eye-opener. And the confidence I felt out there, no matter how heavily the rain was falling and how slippery it all looked, was astounding. Unbelievable. If I learnt nothing else this morning I know how far I can stick my neck out on these tyres. And it's a bloody sight further than I would have guessed.'

Steve Wynne's smile widened as he listened; it was like watching notice being served on Honda, Phil Read and John Williams, that the world title was about to change hands and hemispheres. Mike's happy rain dance on the circuit where his career had taken its first faltering steps twenty years before, was a frisky demonstration of his soaring confidence that he could take up in the Isle of Man where he had left off – winning. Though he was not going to say that for anybody. Not in public, anyway.

In private, it was a different matter. He looked at the TT's entry list and rationalised: 'I know I can win, but I would prefer that people think I have no chance. Then anything more than just a finish is a definite bonus. My best bets must be the Formula One and the 500. The Classic on the 750 is much more of a problem, that'll be Mick's. I can't come to terms with the big Yamaha whatever people keep telling me about its good behaviour and how easy it is easy to ride.'

MIKE THE BIKE – AGAIN

He summed up: 'There are two men to beat, John and Mick. They are experts and they're regular riders; they also want to beat me very badly. I'll reserve all my final judgements until I've had some practice on the island, that's where all the comeuppance starts.'

Ten companies, headed by Martini, sponsored Mike in his TT effort. He was to be a moving placard, a mass of advertising, covered from head to foot, back and front, with endorsements. But he made sure that everybody who had put a pound into the venture had his money's worth of exposure, whatever the demands on his time. Even when, at a test ride session, he was invited by photographers to pose on the Martini-liveried Yamahas he realised his left wrist was bare – so he slipped his on Seiko watch and made sure his leathers were not hiding its easily-identifiable face.

The old days of the black, seal-like leathers, scuffed at the knees and greying at the elbows, looked light years away when the Martini or Sports Motorcycle red, white and gold leathers were yanked over his shoulders in all their multi-coloured and lettered magnificence. But he slipped easily into the role of patient subject, talking well, lucidly and wittily at the sponsors' parties, answering the most inane questions with kindness and smiling through the often irritating twitterings of the fringe people in a way that suggested he was ageing gracefully.

When the time came to pack for the Isle of Man, the long drawn-out test programme had left us content. Mike had been on the threshold of the lap record at Snetterton and at Donington without any effort, the machines seemed to have been on their very best behaviour.

Yamaha mechanic Nobby Clarke promised: 'Baby, there'll be nothing better than the Yams on the island. Nothing. They'll be something special.'

I had arranged for the team to be garaged in what was once Honda's island headquarters, underneath the beach-front Castle Mona Hotel where the lock-up cages were ideal for our purposes. For Nobby, mindful of the need to be security conscious in guarding Yamaha's innermost secrets, had said: 'I don't want anybody looking at those bikes. Nobody. So I don't need any more help than Trevor and Jerry. And if I have to stay up all night I'll strip them down myself when it's necessary. But I am sure Mike will be able to do something on our bikes, the 500 in particular – it'll be a good one.'

Before I left to link up with Mike in the Isle of Man I turned down an offer for him to race as passenger to a well-known sidecar star in the three-wheeler TT ...

The man said: 'It'll create tremendous interest in the TT if he would.' And I replied: 'What do you think has happened already?'

Since the official announcements of Mike's comeback after an eleven-year lay-off, six months before the June date, it had been impossible to get a hotel room or a flight to Ronaldsway, the island's neat little airport, eight miles from Douglas. And a Tourist Board official told me: 'It's all down to Mike's return. We'd have been stuck without him this year. Trade has bucked up no end. The hoteliers are rubbing their hands.'

If we had a worry it was that Mike, having focussed so much attention on the TT, would have a practice spill that put him out of the racing. Obviously, the danger period would be the opening sessions, the times when he was feeling his way once more. But TT organiser Cooper, alert to that problem and alive to Mike's contribution to the TT's well-being in 1978, reassured me: 'If anything should befall Mike, God forbid, I'm sure we'd pay him in full. We've had publicity in plenty, and our money's worth, even now.'

Behind the scenes at ACU headquarters in London they had been hit with a rush of applications from men who wanted to ride in the TT, following in the wake of Mike's comeback. And it had reached embarrassing levels, for there were men who were nowhere near fit enough to compete who demanded licences, citing Mike as an example and suggesting preferential treatment. That, of course, was nonsense. Mike had been competing in races in Australia, even if spasmodically, and it had been only four years since he had raced Formula One cars; the former riders who struggled to get re-licensed had not competed for years at any level. He was also supremely fit, as physically well-honed as any regular athlete and, as his test session times had proved, well able to match the world's top riders on a variety of circuits.

The good news was that both Mick Grant and John Williams were fit and raring to go; Phil Read, too, was eagerly looking forward to his renewed struggle for supremacy against his old foe.

To escape the pressures that were piling up, Mike and his wife went away to a friend's farm in Wiltshire before he was scheduled to fly to the island. Then he delivered Pauline and the children to the home of Richard Attwood, a former Grand Prix car driver who had once won the Le Mans 24-hour race, and whose wife was going to keep Pauline company until after the TT. Richard was to join the team in the Isle of Man –and to bring his unique ability to fall, with wide-eyed and innocent ease, into all sorts of trouble. An arresting quality ...

Mike, joined by Australian Jim Scaysbrook who had been his partner on a Ducati, flew to the island, and found that British Leyland had sent a Rover 3500 across from England for him. An executive who was a fan and a motorcycle race enthusiast thought it might come in useful. And, anyway, the publicity the car would get might be useful ...

A frightening dawn

At the back of everybody's mind lay the glorious probability that Mike would win – the fairy tale that really did seem to be too much to hope for. But while there was a chance, it was important to keep a sense of restraint, to evaluate and balance what needed to be done and what could be done in terms of time available and importance. This was an issue which seemed to escape Barry Briggs, the former world speedway champion – and it rather took me by surprise. I would have expected a little more understanding from him.

He was trying to get a grass track meeting launched as part of what has become a motorcycle festival during TT week, and he wanted – no, he almost demanded – Mike to present the prizes. When I turned down his rather imperiously insistent requests on the basis that, first, Mike had hardly had time to draw breath since he had arrived on the island, and secondly, that on the night he wanted the job doing Mike himself may have been receiving an award at the TT prize presentation ceremony, he was quite miffed.

He reported me to Yamaha headquarters, Amsterdam, and I felt as if I was being paraded before the CO charged with insubordination for pricking somebody's bloated importance. Rod Gould, the Yamaha publicity chief in Europe, added his weight to Briggo's, but I would not be moved. And, as it turned out, Mike did have another date that night ... with some 3,000 people.

But first he had a week of official practice to survive, four machines to try out and to qualify on, and with every non-racing hour a jam of appointments and interviews, life was as hectic as it could be, more than he had ever known in his entire career. We both, I believe, seriously underestimated the magic pull of his name for, as somebody wrote, not one of those people who could not get beds and were sleeping on the beach would have been the least bit surprised to see Mike walk ashore from the Irish Sea.

He was happiest when he was riding; it was the only time he had any peace from the claustrophobic atmosphere his own popularity generated. He learned to live with it – though, at times, his patience must have been sorely tried.

Even before the first official practice he had completed about 30 laps of the course in a car or on a road machine. Nothing, therefore, came as a surprise to him. The valuable 'lappery' building up to the TT, coupled with the familiarisation progress he had made at the Manx Grand Prix in September, had keyed him up superbly. I could detect in him an impatience to get down to the serious business; he was sleeping well, he was eating sparingly and drinking nothing alcoholic, and he was in a vibrant mood. He knew he was ready; he knew he was equal to the challenge; only the machinery, or some freak happening, could alter that.

We had dinner with Mick Grant and it turned into a four-hour teach-in on the TT, the new TT so far as Mike was concerned. He listened as intently as would any genuinely fascinated man. Mick told him he was in top gear on his big Kawasaki only seven or eight times on each lap.

'Steadiness, Mike, that's the clue now,' he stressed, 'absolute steadiness. Every lap the same. 8,000 revs maximum – then change. I don't want you to think I'm trying to teach you how to do it, but that's the way to win here these days.

'Who'll win? Aside from one of us here? Well, I think it'll be John Williams. Willy is so good here. So good. He's always a handful. Joey Dunlop? No. He won't find it as easy as he did last year. No chance.

'Tom Herron? He's great at the North West 200, but it's not the same here. He'll have his work cut out, too.' Herron, in fact, had just flown to the island from Ireland where he had shattered the lap record at the North West 200 with a new high of 127.63mph – but then, with a tyre fast falling apart under the incredible speeds, he had been forced to slow down until he had dropped into sixth place. Tony Rutter won at a record average of 124.76mph, faster even than John Williams' lap record. The chase for TT honours was hotting up.

Later Mike said: 'Mick confirmed everything that I had been thinking about the TT and how to tackle it. It's the other guys I've got to fathom now.' We sat for two hours poring over the entry list, assessing each main challenger's strong and weak points until we had narrowed down the field to a fast few, who we honestly believed would give the biggest resistance.

'Oh, by the way, I was nearly off today,' he said as casually as he could. 'Jim Scaysbrook rammed me.' I still had my hand clapped to my forehead when he went on: 'He was following me round on a road bike when a sheep ran out in front of me and I had to slam the brakes on.

'Jim was dozing along behind me, gawping at a bloke digging in a field, and he didn't see what had happened until it was almost too late. He banged into the back of my bike and we were both nearly off. It was a close thing, and I was as near to coming down as you could be without hitting the deck. Otherwise everything seems to be going fine, slotting into place nicely and by the time official practice starts I'll be good and ready to get in a good few fast laps.

'I'm just getting a bit edgy now, a little uptight, but it's a good thing for me. I like to feel that way because I know that when it comes to hey-lads-hey I'll be ready.

'Do you have any ideas where I can get a false moustache? Dark glasses and an astronaut's cap aren't enough of a disguise and it's getting a bit embarrassing now: I daren't set foot outside my bedroom, even here in the hotel, without a crowd gathering.

'I suppose I should be grateful in one way, and I'm more than a little surprised just how hectic it gets, but I can't ever get used to it. What bugs me is that people don't recognise my need to be left alone at times – mainly when I'm eating or talking to friends or discussing business. It doesn't make any difference, some folk just come barging in. They refuse to respect privacy or even follow normal rules of good manners and behaviour.

'Some guy even followed me into the loo to ask me for an autograph! Beat that. Others are nicer, of course. Like the guy this afternoon who wheeled up his little lad – about four he was – and produced a birth certificate for me to sign. I thought I'd been accused of something I hadn't done until he explained he'd called his lad after me ... Stanley Michael Bailey ... and would I autograph the certificate. The little boy had no more idea who I was than I know who invented the wheel. Strange, though, isn't it?'

The fact that official practice had been reduced to a total of only six hours worried Mike somewhat. He felt it was not enough and became determined, so far as he could, to get some extra time built into the week with an early morning session, if the ACU would agree.

He told me: 'Everything is so different these days, I found out that much in the test sessions we've had before I came to the island.

'The tyres and brakes for instance, there's so much stopping power and grip compared with 1967 that it's like a totally new sport. I've not only got to re-learn the circuit and the changes in its surface at racing speeds, I've got to learn how to ride again.

'Six hours' official practice may sound a long time, but when you remember I've got four bikes to take round a circuit that's 37 and a bit miles it works out at one and a half hours a machine! Not much, is it? And that's not making any allowances for problems that could arise, stops for adjustments and unforeseen problems.

'And these modern racing bikes! They're so bloody uncomfortable – they're built for riders who sit much farther forward than pleases me. I had to have the seats moved back a couple of inches or so and the handlebars altered, too, so that I could ride without getting cramped up. Comfort, at my time of life, is an absolute essential. And this can be a very uncomfortable race at times, two hours or so of sheer agony if you're not careful. As I'm planning to stay the distance I'd like to make sure all is to my liking.'

Just before first practice Phil Read and his lovely new wife, Angie, called to see Mike at his hotel. The two men sat in the hot sunshine, Mike stripped down to trunks, Read in slacks and sports shirt, and traded chat about their chances. And Phil bemoaned the Honda set-up, a man plainly unhappy with his lot despite being favourite for the race he had won the year before. Mike, happily, had no such problems, and despite his edginess he was looking forward to putting Steve Wynne's pride and joy through its paces. The Ducati, he reckoned, was just right for the rigours it faced; not the best machine for a short circuit struggle, but perfect for the TT. And he could hardly wait.

We went for a last look on four wheels at the course and, particularly, the descent from Snaefell, that high rise in the middle of the circuit where the fog or the wind could be perfidy personified. And we met Tom Herron on a road machine, to-ing and fro-ing around the 32nd milestone, a difficult, elongated bend centred in a series of left-handers.

We stopped the Rover and Mike sent the windows sliding down at the touch of the electric button. Tom shoved his helmeted head into the car and in that Irish burr of his pleaded: 'Mike, do you have any idea how to get round this bloody bend? I've been trying all week and I don't know.'

'I've been trying since 1959 and I've still no idea, and I'll know no better by the end of the TT,' he replied.

'Well, that's all right,' said Tom, 'we'll blunder round it together. At least I know you won't make any time up on me here.' 'The way you've been riding lately,' said Mike, 'I won't make any time on you anywhere.'

Tom, as cheery as ever, grinned at the compliment and enjoyed the warmth of Mike's remark. He set off back for Douglas – and was stopped by the police for speeding. He was later fined £17 with £2 costs, and in TT week, when the Chief Constable of the Isle of Man asked him for an autograph in the Martini hospitality marquee, Tom quipped: 'Aye, but it'll cost you £19 ...'

In 1977 one of the greatest of the TT riders was stopped by the police in Douglas, the island's capital, for drunken driving. It was early in the morning and he was swinging his eye-catching foreign car through the long bend when he was spotted by a policeman, chased and stopped.

The young officer, obviously not a TT fan, had no idea of the identity of his catch until they got back to the police station, where it was pointed out to him by a senior officer.

The internationally famous ace – not noted for any great drinking prowess – was sent back to his hotel. He raced the next day with great success, and no action was taken by the police against a man who was much the most popular of all time at the TT.

By the time practice week got under way Mike was at a peak – he was down to 11 stone, half a stone heavier than his racing weight in 1967, and felt strong enough to go twice the distance he was going to have to race. But he did not find himself convinced he could win anything until the Friday evening before the first race of the week, Saturday 3 June's Formula One event ...

MIKE THE BIKE – AGAIN

He had his eyes glued on the massive winged Mercury trophy for the Formula One race – it used to be the prize for the 125cc race – and felt that if there was any hope for him, it would come in that class. But he could not have had a worse or more demoralising start to rehearsals for the big show ...

The flame-coloured Ducatis lined up in the parc ferme behind the grandstand looked splendid, an impressive array of sparkling machinery, superbly prepared, fussed over like newborn babies – and just about as noisy. Indeed, if there was any doubt about them it had to be whether they would get through the decibel test, but they did. And I'll never know how, though it would have been a crime to have muffled the marvellously exciting throatiness.

Despite his vast experience, Mike was as nervous as anybody in the hurly-burly of the paddock; it was all noise and smoke, colour and confusion, with fleeting smiles, edgy remarks and a lot of last-minute instruction being yelled into ears under helmets to minds that were miles away. There is more than one sort of deafness at the TT ...

Mike was no different; he had been this way before. Often. With a record of twelve TT wins between 1961 and 1967, and lap records set almost every year, there should have been nothing new to him. But it was all new, he was starting again and the mantrap that faced him was the gap of years. The cause of his deafness was his concentration and his awareness of the weighty responsibility on his shoulders. It was too late for talking; it was time for action. And, as Mick Grant had said earlier in the week, 'We'll wait until practice to see how good he is, how much of his skill he has lost, and whether he can come back with a win. Any other way is just useless speculation.' Grant has a way of summing up the situation succinctly – and Mike has his own way of replying.

But his first attempt took him no further than a humble few miles down the road in the first practice session; to a pub, 'The Crosby.' It was outside there that the sleekly efficient Ducati spluttered and, uncharacteristically, came to a dead halt.

A knot of curious spectators gathered around Mike as he tried to puzzle out what had sabotaged his first gallop on the F1 mount.

'And you know me – what I know about motor bikes you could write on the back of a postage stamp and still have room,' he laughed later, 'so I was really stuck. It was so bloody frustrating and I was really annoyed. The air was blue and I just about ripped that bike apart.

'I tore everything I could off it. The saddle, the lot ... I fiddled with the wiring, the battery and checked everything that looked as if it might carry electricity. But it was still a mystery to me and, aside from stand there and scratch my head, there was nothing I could do.'

There were some ghostly white faces back in the Ducati enclosure at the grandstand. A chalked notice had appeared on the blackboard nailed onto the incidents hut alongside the paddock, and it announced that number 12 – Mike's number for all his four races – had stopped at

Crosby. Steve Wynne, John Sear and Pat Slinn, the Sports Motorcycles men, watched the colour drain from each other's faces and then hurried to their van to collect the machine and bring it back to the start and finish area.

In the meantime Mike hitched a lift with a man on his way to play in a cricket match; he had left the Ducati propped in a hedge by the side of the road and was in a desperate rush to try and salvage some practice time from what was left of the session. And while Steve and his men pondered the problem Mike set off for his first ride on the 500cc Yamaha. That, at least, went without incident and by the time he had returned the Ducati snag had been ironed out. The Lucas Rita ignition transistor box had failed, probably because of vibration – the first time anybody could recall that happening. A new box and battery were fitted and Mike flew back into the fray.

When he headed back into the Ducati enclosure I had him clocked as having unofficially broken Phil Read's one-year-old lap record; confirmation came later. He had – with a speed of 102.69mph compared with the standing record of 101.74mph. He was not only top in that session, but he nosed in front of the rest in the 500cc class, too. His speed was 105.70, marginally ahead of Tom Herron who was given 105.47mph.

Herron told me: 'You've nothing to worry about with the old man, he's going so well it's a pleasure to see him. I'd put money on him winning something, he's lost nothing of his old flair – and he's so smooth and safe looking. He came by me when I thought I was going very well. It could only have been one man. I was into a corner when he came by, almost sat up and swept through it beautifully, and was away like a shot out of a gun. You can learn something new just by watching him at times like that.'

It was a happier, more relaxed Mike back at the hotel. 'I feel tons better now. Let's have a glass of red wine to celebrate,' he offered.

I went away for a 'phone call and returned to find a drunk hovering and swaying over Mike as he tried to eat his dinner: he was being embarrassingly laudatory and over-enthusiastic; a downright nuisance who could not take the hint that he had outstayed his welcome. Mike did not want to make a scene and, in the end, I had to show him the way out.

The conversation centred on the circuit, with little or no mention of the men he would have to beat – not yet, anyway. And Mike said: 'The racing is going to be a terrific test of mental stamina; but then it always was.

'Physical fitness is one aspect, naturally, but the need to be alert and to have one's concentration switched on to an absolute pitch is vital. And that really takes it out of you here. The TT is one race where you cannot afford to relax for a second – carelessness can be fatal, there are so many pitfalls for the unwary. It's such a hell of a long way round, with so many changes of condition, that you've just got to be with it all the way. Then the machines are so incredibly fast you get no time at all to think things out, you've got to be right first time. Any hesitation, any doubt anywhere, when you're heading for a corner at the speeds they take you is fatal. That's why I've been so determined to put in as many laps in the car and on the road bike as I possibly could. Not one second of that time has been wasted.

'There are lines now – and Mick Grant pointed them out to me when we went out together in my car – that weren't there for me when I last raced the big Honda here in 1967. They are totally different now; the tyres, so much improved, the vastly different brakes and the handling of the bikes, gives you a whole range of problems that didn't exist before.

'The section that has changed most of all in the eleven years I've been away is over the mountain ... the Black Hut, the Verandah and the Bungalow. That's the most noticeable aspect of change; there are, of course, many other bits that have been altered, but they're not so obvious as that stretch.

'As far as Ballacraine from the start the road is marvellous, the surface good and smooth, but then it always was. At Union Mills they've taken away an entire bend – and up to Creg Willys hill, the section where Agostini and I both fell off in 1964, the surface is really smooth and it's the same up to the Cronk-y-Voddy straight – but it's by no means ideal. The surface is smooth okay – but then it suddenly gives way to a terribly bumpy bit where the new bit ends and joins the old surface. And if you don't anticipate it and start braking before the crossroads there, where it's really bad, you can be in all sorts of trouble.'

His almost yard-by-yard description of the course, its new difficulties, its old problems, and the sections where he felt he could or could not make up time, was based on the painstaking examination of it in the build-up to practice week. It went through his mind like a print-out.

His only worry, he said, was that people were taking his reappearance at the TT much more seriously than he had originally intended. 'It's been built into something far bigger than I had anticipated and it's worrying. I just wanted to come back and enjoy myself without being bothered where I finished, but now I can sense that everybody's rooting for me and it's a lot of pressure to withstand. I've a horror of letting people down.

'I'm afraid that it'll all be too much and too fast for my poor old brain to cope with; so you can see I don't want to have anything to think about aside from the racing. But I can't avoid it.'

He had more than enough to think about with the Yamahas, particularly the 250. It would not behave itself and in the end, having suffered its misfires and gearbox problems, and having struggled to master the art of starting it, Mike logged only two practice laps on it. The big 750, too, gave him some anxious moments – not only because of its immense power ...

He went in among the slower Formula Two and Formula Three bikes in midweek practice but the Yamaha 750 ate up a piston as he motored, again, towards Crosby. There was an awful metallic graunching and he quickly snapped in the clutch to coast to a halt at the pub, where he was fast becoming a regular. Once more he lost valuable practice time, though he was more worried about the antics of much slower men on the course.

He told me: 'Some of the riding is criminal, slower men all over the place, wandering about as if they don't have any idea where they are. And it's no fun when you're coming up on them at around 100 miles-an-hour quicker. It's not their fault, really, the F2 and F3 guys shouldn't have been mixed in with the faster men. It's too dangerous for words and there are crashes all over the place. It's all you can do to stay clear of trouble.

He was not a happy man. He wanted to get in a flyer of a lap. 'It's important right now,' he explained, 'to get a psychological advantage over the rest and get in a really good lap. Put 'em off a bit. Make them think they've not got it all their own way. But with this trouble it's impossible, and that's not the way I like things to go.'

It was clear to everybody around him that Mike was, by now, enjoying complete confidence in his own ability. It was the machines that failed to match his ambitions for them. He had set his own limitations – and they were high, even if, as he said repeatedly, they would stop at about 80 per cent of his comfortable skill level.

It was this reassurance from him that I constantly asked for – and if it became boringly repetitious it was because I felt the need to remind him that just so much effort was all that would be required provided the machinery lived up to our hopes. There was, of course, no guaranteeing what would happen once the flag dropped and the adrenalin began to flood the arteries, but I felt there had to be some outside conditioning of Mike's attitude at as long a distance from the actual race as feasible. Nobody close to him had any doubts at all that he was going to be leaving the island a winner – but the chance that he might take a risk too many to achieve it had to be wiped out. We were driving to the circuit for the last-but-one practice session, on the Ducati, when I mentioned it to him again and he said: 'I'm going to throw the gauntlet down – but, I promise, I'll take it easy. Don't worry. Don't WORRY!'

When the session was finished he had lapped at 111.04mph on the slimline Italian twin – an astonishing high, with Tom Herron's Honda second at 109.27mph and Phil Read's works Honda at 109.18mph. It seemed to me that the Formula One race had been won and lost right there: I was sure Herron could not have gone much quicker and Phil certainly did not relish anything faster.

It was the quickest Mike had ever lapped but he did not stretch himself at all. 'I wasn't even trying too hard,' he said, 'I just took it nice and easy. And it was no problem at all.

'This is the first moment, really, that I have genuinely believed I can win. I've kept my hopes and my feelings in check and just gone about the job as thoroughly as I can, but right now I know I can win.

'I wanted to see how fast I could go without sticking my neck out and just to make sure the bike was okay. When I got going it all just fitted nicely into place.

'I did a warm-up lap and then, as I told you, I thought I'd throw the gauntlet down. Everything went exactly as I planned, no hitches, no scares, no problems at all. In fact, it went so smoothly I thought I may have done around 106 miles-an-hour, it felt like only that sort of speed. I was knocked out when I was told it was 111mph, because there was so much left. I had plenty in hand, but I gather it's just about Phil's limit on the Honda.' There were a good few other riders at the TT who would have considered that the 38-year-old veteran's lap was more than enough for them to contend with, riders who would have been happy to claim that they could have got round at five miles-an-hour less. Whatever the final figure, it was the way he had done it that was more important. With effort, sure, but without any trace of strain or overreaching either himself or the machine.

His lap time was a mountain for the others to climb – but there was even more to come and, surprisingly, from the area where he had the greatest apprehensions and doubts ... from the Classic entry, the 750 superbike, the 190-mile-an-hour Yamaha. First, though, there was a scare to survive, as close to being disastrous as we could get.

It was almost like falling into a snare he had set for himself; he had been active in trying to get an extra practice session and had succeeded in making the ACU officials see the sense of the request. They agreed to organise one for solos early on the morning of the Formula One race, and shortly after dawn Mike and a handful of other riders who could be bothered took advantage of the bonus practice. Anyway, with a race coming up later that day, it was doubly valuable for competitors who could not afford to miss out on any chance to see the circuit at racing speeds.

It was a sleepy Hailwood who answered his 4am alarm call, hauled on his leathers and then knocked me up so that we could join the rest of the team in the chill, grey gloom of the start and finish area.

Dawn practice is a terrible shock to the system, and an even bigger one to somebody like Mike who does not sleep at all well at the best of times; there are red-rimmed eyes and yawns, seagulls screeching enough to make your head buzz, and that all-pervading cold that ghosts in under the warmest anorak and leathers and refrigerates the bones. The only shield from it is a rider's enthusiasm and eagerness, an antidote of warmth of effort.

The roulette wheels were spinning as freely as the heads of the drunks, and the randier dancers in the Casino's disco were locked in a ritual embrace as Mike, rolling plugs for his ears and snapping on the visors to an ill-fitting helmet, listened to South African mechanic Trevor Tilbury intoning: 'Don't forget, new tyre on the front. Take it easy. New tyre to scrub in. All right?'

Trevor, looking after the 250, had meddled with the needles so that Mike, who had suffered all sorts of troubles trying to get it to fire up, found it easier to start. He smiled contentedly when the little lightweight, something of a nuisance, really, in our plan of campaign for the TT, buzzed into life and Mike lazily lifted his right leg across the saddle and settled in for what he hoped might be a useful, if not out of the ordinary lap, on the smallest of our machines.

'Everything was fine,' said Mike, 'aside from the very idea of riding so early in the morning, even though I knew it was essential, and I had come to terms with the inevitability of it all. I'd much rather have been having a flutter or a jig back at the hotel but ... work was work.

'I was well aware of Trevor's warning – he said it often enough – about the new tyre on the front and the need to take it easy until it was scrubbed in. And I did. I took it extremely slowly.

'When I got to Braddan Bridge, the left and right past the church, I was still going nice and easy. But the front wheel skidded on that shiny little patch in the middle of the bridge, the front went away (and I've never found anybody who corrected one of those), and I was on my backside. The bike clouted the wall and the petrol tank separated from its moorings.

'I felt so bloody stupid and, I'll admit, extremely shaken. It was the first fright I'd had all week – and it had to come on race day! Well, it did me no good and, at the same time, a lot of good. I realised that even I could fall off when I wasn't even sticking my neck out. Few people believed me, but I really wasn't going fast. I know all about the dangers of new tyres and I was determined not to be trapped. So much for my determination!

'When I picked myself up and had a look round to make sure nobody had seen me to add to my embarrassment, I could see the funny side of it.

'I stood there, my fingers hurting like mad and bleeding, and imagined all your faces, the rest of the team, back at the grandstand waiting for me to come back round again. Not funny, really, because I knew I was okay, but you lot back there wouldn't know what the hell was going on.'

In fact, the controller of the incidents hut sought me out in the crowd in the paddock and whispered: 'Mike's off at Braddan, we think he's okay. But I won't put his number up on the board now you know.' My face was white enough – but it wasn't enough for Mike. His wicked sense of humour sent him scurrying to his car, after he had hitched a lift back from Braddan, to put on a joke bandaged and bleeding finger. He held it up as he came towards me: 'Well, that's it. Finished. The thing's broken. All that work for nothing ... 'He had done the same once before, 'phoning me at home saying he was in hospital with a busted leg, and then ending up full of remorse.

We wanted him to go to hospital anyway to have an X-ray on his hand, for it had swollen up pretty spectacularly, but he resisted. His anger was acute, directed at nobody but himself, and that self-admonishment was misdirected, I felt. But he was inconsolable once he had recovered from the nasty dent in his invincibility.

(It is ironic that after racing for so many years on the threshold, and survived, on two wheels, that Mike's obvious injuries stem from car crashes.

MIKE THE BIKE – AGAIN

His curiously bent leg, the legacy of his horrifying F1 pile-up, and the pinch of flesh under his left eye, the result of a collision with a cow on open roads in South Africa when the roof of his Ferrari was thrown back by the impact, are the only outward signs of a brush with death.)

He said: 'It could have all gone by the board this morning. Everything we had done and planned, all the money that people have put in as support, could have been wasted. I am so lucky I wasn't hurt any more than a couple of scratches. It was a good reminder that motorcycle racing IS dangerous and it CAN hurt, even when you are taking it nice and steady.' Nice and steady? I wondered if his nice and steady was the same as everybody else's. 'It certainly is,' he replied, 'because there was no point in going quick. The 250 bike was not our priority, it was a make-weight. And there was no way I was going to do anything daft on it.'

Practice week had not been without its dramas. When Mike had taken out the 500cc Senior mount – our second hope for a win – he had complained about its handling. And it must have been really bad, because he did not usually fuss too much about a machine's waywardness, unless it was particularly naughty.

'It's all over the place,' he told mechanic Nobby Clarke, 'and I can't fathom it.' Nobby soon discovered the problem. When he took the fuel tank off he found the frame was split, two downtubes behind the steering stock had come adrift and it was swinging loose. Frame expert Ken Sprayson fixed it – but with that, a badly knocked-about 250 and an OW31 that had suffered a regular misfire and had once gone, in Mike's words, 'as flat as a kipper,' the mechanics were not getting what would have been considered a trade union norm of sleep. Tilbury, working all night, snatched catnaps in the back of the van rather than leave the job and go back to the hotel. Nobby, too, taking leave from Kenny Roberts' world title campaign, spent less time sleeping than on his Grand Prix beat. Jerry Wood and his girlfriend spent all their time ferreting for parts and ferrying them here, there, and everywhere.

But whatever labour had gone into the build-up, this last day of practice wiped away the weariness totally; it was reward in itself for everybody concerned with the team. After Mike's final run on the Ducati, when he had thrown down the gauntlet and bettered Phil Read's one-year-old lap record by nearly ten miles an hour, the Yamaha men were looking for him to prove that their efforts had not been in vain. Nobody said it, but Mike felt it. And the need, too, to show the opposition, Mick Grant in particular, that the Classic race for superbikes was not going to go all the way of the Yorkshireman.

The 250cc crash served only to put a finer edge on Mike's performance that day. And when the handsome-looking Yamaha superbike was wheeled out, dressed head to tail in the Martini livery, Mike's feeling, despite his dislike for the bike and his uneasiness aboard it, was one of desire to triumph over doubt.

It was a perfect morning, clear and bright. The needle on the rev counter flickered under Nobby's grip and the bike crackled crisply in obedient response. It looked and it sounded like the perfect counter to Grant's Kawasaki, the machine that, a year before, had taken him through the TT radar trap at 191mph; and with Mike on his toes and impatient to get going, this practice session, the last one of all, promised to be as good as any race.

As it turned out, the Classic practice was indeed more exciting than the race proper. Mainly because Mike's big Yamaha lasted longer in training than it did in the race, and Grant felt the full force of his powerful riding.

When Mike pushed away from the line under the timekeepers' hut he was confident he could match Mick's dash; even with the 750 misfiring and spluttering on three cylinders for the final 17 miles of one practice session on it he had logged a lap of around 111mph. Now it was back to a peak of readiness, after so much hard labour by the mechanics, and he wanted to put it through the hoop.

Grant, who pushed off just behind him, told me later: 'Being with him was the highlight of the TT for me that year. He was already a well-established star on the Grand Prix scene when I started my career and was wobbling around club circuits. So Mike had always been a hero to me. And I'd been in the same race as him only once before – Silverstone, 1972. A 350 event.

'I was just in behind the leaders when this lunatic in a red helmet came hurtling by me to join the front runners: I couldn't believe it. I had no idea who the guy was.

'I couldn't recognise the helmet at all – but it was one he had borrowed. So he was totally unrecognisable. Anyway, it didn't take me too long to figure that it could only be one man ... Hailwood. And that was the last I saw of him in that race. He had been retired from motor bike racing for a while. Somebody persuaded him to race at Silverstone as a one-off, but he couldn't get the bike going from the start and had been left on the line. But he finished third ... amazing!

'So, until we went away together at that last practice session in 1978, I had never been up against him in serious competition ... and you can't count that brief flash of him I had at Silverstone.

'When you race against men of Mike's class you know you can trust them implicitly and can get as close as you like without feeling you are approaching any danger – and that's the way I felt that morning as I tucked in behind him. I wasn't out to see what he could do, though I thought he might have been foxing in practice earlier on, I was just going to go at my own tempo. As it turned out Mike wasn't in a mood to hang about so it was obvious it was going to be interesting.

'There were no surprises for me going down Bray Hill, into and out of Quarter Bridge and Braddan, where I could see he was settling down nicely, or even through Union Mills. It was all nice and quick and very smooth, and I was really impressed.

'We were knocking on a bit going to Ballacraine, that sharp right-hander, and suddenly Mike sat up and grabbed his brake. I wondered what the bloody hell was happening, I thought he'd seized – he was so far short of the corner's braking point I was sure he was in trouble. It took me so much by surprise I came as close as anything to ramming him.

'And it kept happening. We'd be going along at a good lick, I'd be tucked in, head down, knees in the fairing, right behind him and then, suddenly, up he'd sit, thirty yards short of the corner, and I'd be nearly bumping into him again. It took me some time to realise that he had no idea of braking points. It had been eleven years since he'd raced on the island and he was still using his 1967 braking marks.

'He was riding as if the machine still had drum brakes, and here we were on the most sophisticated discs, the best stoppers you could get.

'With my brakes I could almost go past the corner, brake, and still get round without any problems at all. Mike, not being used to them, couldn't get it right. He might as well have been riding without any brakes at all, he was knocking it off so far from the corner, braking and then sort of flopping into the bend.

'His riding was wonderful to see. And it suddenly dawned on me just how good his riding had been all week if his braking was so bad. There was nothing spectacular about it, just perfect steadiness, despite his eleven-year-old lines, and a neatness you don't see too often these days. Aside from that his control was superb, everything in the correct sequence and so well balanced. His fault with the braking was something that could easily be put right – he had no other weaknesses at all and was so bloody quick it was marvellous to see how his natural ability coped with the dramatic change that he must surely have felt in the machinery.

'But there's something more, too. His sense of destiny and direction, so highly developed, must go a long way. His mind must have been almost like a computer – nothing, I could see, that the circuit presented could surprise him. He was good at everything, bad at nothing. Except his braking, and that was due to the passing of time and his not being used to what was the most advanced improvement since his racing days.

'I have always been able to get through the twisty bits, from the start to Ramsey, without any problems, as good as the best, but I wanted to follow Mike over the mountain. That's my weak point at the TT. So I stayed tucked in behind ...

'But when we got to Ramsey hairpin Mike, the rotten bugger, waved me on. And I couldn't refuse. He'd led all the way so I had to take my turn up front. And I made a mess of everything over the top, I couldn't get it right at all. But it was still so enjoyable, even though I knew right there and then that I'd met my match, as good as I was at the Isle of Man. It was evident from the way he had motored that he was the man to beat in my big race, the Classic.

'He was obviously going to be the man to beat in the Formula One later that afternoon AND the Senior, too. There was no doubt in my mind that he was a handful to anybody, even to those of us who were racing regularly, week in and week out. His natural skill overcame any rustiness he may have had. But I couldn't get over how he had got round so quickly, 11 years after racing on the island, without good braking points and on machinery worlds apart from that which he used to ride. All of it underlined to me just what a genius of a rider he was.

'I could not imagine what he must have been like in the '60s and it was crazy to me, sad to him I'm sure, that he retired, or was forced to, when he was right at the peak of his form and fitness in 1967. How many world titles over and above the ten he won would he have clinched if he'd gone on, instead of turning to cars?

'I sat thinking these things in the bath when I got back to my hotel. I must admit I was a bit down in the dumps, too. I heard that Pat Hennen had gone around at 113 on his 500 Suzuki and, he said, he hadn't stretched himself beyond eight-tenths.

'I know that neither Mike nor I overreached ourselves either: I was sure I could have done 113 as well. But then Manx Radio announced that I had done over 113, and it made my week. I didn't feel at all troubled doing that sort of speed and I knew then that if necessary – but only if necessary – I could go up to 115mph.'

Mike's view of his morning's joust with Classic favourite Grant was: 'He wasn't half on some funny lines, off the road a couple of times, but his braking was bloody good.'

We both thought that the pressure Mike had put on Mick over Snaefell mountain had pushed him into high areas of speeds where, first he was not happy to be, and second, he was not prepared to go again.

'At times,' said Mike, 'Mick's line was really weird and his braking needed to be good. Whether it was because I was behind him I'm not sure. But I think I've got his measure now.

'When I waved him on I wasn't sure who it was behind me, but I was glad to follow him to see how he tackled the mountain. I was delighted to see he was just as bad as I am over there.

'I know my braking was desperate stuff. Terrible. But I just couldn't get it right. I was far too early, far too heavy. So I had to make it up on the swervy and flat-out bits. I was still operating the brake points I'd had in 1967 and it was no good at all – but even though I was having to ride hard I was nowhere near the limit, not at any stage at all.

'I had so much in hand it did me a world of good to know that hard as Mick seemed to be trying I kept him in sight; he didn't lose me at all.

'I felt nicely jacked up when I was told I'd got round at 112.36, the gratifying aspect being that it had been no problem whatever with no frights at all.'

Thus, it was a supremely confident Mike who napped through the morning of Saturday 3 June, faced later that afternoon with the formidable barrier of Phil Read to clear, in order to take up where he had left off in the Isle of Man 11 years before. Winning …

A fairy tale comes true

The knock on my hotel bedroom door was much earlier than I had expected, by half an hour in fact. But I was ready to go anyway. I had been sitting on my bed staring out over the glistening Irish Sea and wondering what the afternoon would bring. It was Formula One day, Mike's strongest chance for a win in a week where the eyes of the racing world were focussed not only on one place, but on one man – Mike. And the day was good.

When Mike's knuckles had rapped me out of my daydreaming I found him standing in the corridor ready to go. The red, white and gold leathers were already on, but half hidden under an anorak, and his red, white and gold helmet was jammed under his arm. His face was a mould of determination and seriousness: 'Right, let's go. Let's get up there.'

The Ducati, his workhorse for the afternoon, was already in the paddock area, being stared at, fussed over, polished and checked and re-checked. Its fairing looked like an advertising hoarding – but then Mike's chest, too, was a moving placard.

The car journey up the long hill from the hotel was a pretty laconic ten minutes, through Nobles Park and into the grandstand area, where the gateman, immediately recognising the familiar profile in the silver Rover, stepped aside and waved Mike straight through.

'Read. What about him? Do you think he can go any quicker?' he asked, and waited for the negative reply. 'And John Williams. He's so bloody good here. Can he do it do you think?' The answer from me was the same: 'I don't think either one of them can beat you. And I think you scared the pants off them with that 111-mile-an-hour practice time. Phil doesn't want to have to be going round that quick – and he's your main threat. He and John Willy both know you weren't even trying when you did that time.'

Phil had, in fact, clocked a lap of 109.18 in Formula One practice but, as he told me later, it was in sheer temper. He was having so much trouble and discontent behind the scenes with Honda and with his hotel that he took it out on the machine.

'I really let off all my steam,' he said. 'I just made that thing go as fast as I could. And I was chuffed when I found I had done a lap that quick. But my feeling was that I didn't want to have to go much faster in the actual race.' So, indeed, Phil had virtually shot his bolt.

Armed with this information, Mike was a confident man as he parked his car: he had figured out that the plus factors of the Ducati allied to the minus factors of the other runners and their machines had propelled him forward as favourite in his own mind. He had decided to attack from the beginning, from the moment the race got under way. It was a tactic that had paid off so handsomely for him many times before at the TT – a blistering opening lap, an appraisal of the whereabouts of the opposition after the two-by-two staggered start of the race, and then a consolidation of his position if he was satisfied with this progress.

I had arranged that Mike ran under the number 12 – the number of TTs he had won up to then – a handy starting position with all the quicker men ahead of him, and Phil Read, the reigning champion, setting off as number 1.

And when Phil, Mike's Grand Prix rival of the '60s and a world champion eight times, rocketed the big Honda away from the line, crouched snugly behind the screen and headed down the helter skelter of the awesome Bray Hill, the Ducati had 50 seconds to wait. An interminable length of time, it seemed. Too much to make up for a sight of the slim, red-leathered Read. But Mike was cool, or at least he looked it. He admitted later that his mind was a turmoil of apprehension, and his stomach churning.

The throaty growl of the Italian four-stroke disguised its sleek surge – it was always going faster than it sounded – and Mike roared in pursuit of the front runners, Read in particular. There was an historical rivalry between them, old scores to settle and, for Mike, a world title to be pinched from Phil.

Steve Wynne watched the back of the Ducati distance itself from the starter's flag, bob like a hare's tail on the run, and finally swing out of sight, though not out of sound, over the crest of Bray, under the footbridge and into the gaze of the first bunch of excited spectators gathered by the trackside. Then he walked with his paraphernalia of spanners towards his allotted pit box.

He began his 100-yard walk, trying not to look too keyed up, as Mike began to gobble the first of the 226 miles that stood between him and the most emotional TT in the long and dramatic history of the races. They were two men separated for the next two hours by choice of vocation, joined together by a concern for each other's skill and a determination to win, and linked by the belief that Mike could do it.

Up in the press box I had a telephone line open to Mike's wife, Pauline, staying with friends in Wolverhampton. And all around me eyes were glued onto the progress clocks on the scoreboard directly opposite the grandstand, whose jerky fingers pointed to four stages of each of the six laps, indicating when a rider had safely passed. The fascination they normally held for spectators soon became almost redundant, because within eight miles of the start Mike had taken over the lead in the race, and all eyes were on him.

MIKE THE BIKE – AGAIN

Read had gone off at a blistering rate but, as we had worked out from his practice and his subsequent feelings, he had not reached even his training speeds. Irishman Tom Herron, who had managed a lap of 109.27 in practice, was looking threatening.

Mike, trying to make up that 50-second leeway separating him and Read on the road, did not manage it for a lap and a half, but I do not suppose there was a soul gathered around the island's most famous 37¾ miles of road who did not believe it was inevitable. Even Read himself knew it, and he was trying all he knew to postpone it.

When the field streamed like a multi-coloured snake past the grandstand, and when the timekeepers had finished the monumental job of calculating the times of around 100 riders, the picture that began to appear was the one just about everybody in the world of racing wanted to see, but dare not hope would emerge.

Mike, gloriously, wonderfully, was in front by about nine seconds. Ranged behind him, baffled by his genius and on the way to being defeated by his unfathomable skill, was a huffing, puffing, panting group of regular, week-in-week-out riders struggling to catch the man who had not raced the TT for 11 years. A 38-year-old veteran, crippled in a car crash but stirred to unbeatable heights by a will to win that flowed through him as vitally as the blood that tingled with adrenalin.

There was Grand Prix regular John Williams, the 500cc lap record holder; Charles Mortimer, a world title contender in a GP class of his own; Helmut Dahne, the BMW works rider, a TT expert; Alex George, another world championship star; Read, of course, who with Williams was on full works machinery; and a collection of hard riders who would be difficult to beat in any circumstances. But none had the measure of Mike. The years just rolled off him.

At the end of the first lap he had logged an opening 37¾ miles in 20m 36.2s, a speed of 109.87mph. Herron, on the privately owned Mocheck-Honda, as fast a monster of machinery as there was in the race, had a time of 20m 45.0s, a speed of 109.09mph. Read was in third place, fighting desperately but vainly, with a time of 20m 56.6s and a lap speed of 108.09mph, and he was almost at his ceiling. Fourth was his teammate John Williams, the likeable Liverpool Honda rider drafted into the team on a one-off contract. He had clocked 21m 16.6s, a speed of 106.39mph. Behind him, in fifth place, was Ian Richards with 21m 17.2s, a speed of 106.34mph. And in sixth place was German Helmut Dahne.

The tall, elegant German's figures were 21m 21.4s on his opening burst – a speed of 106.00mph. The cold figures of Mike's progress could be traced to Ian Richards, the man who set off paired with Mike. He was some 40 seconds down on the maestro by the end of the first lap, and even though he kept on going hard it was going to develop into an even wider margin.

Halfway around the second lap, approaching the island's second town, Ramsey, Mike and the massive crowd assembled there got exactly

70

what they had yearned for – Read and Hailwood within yards of each other. Read burst from the shadows of the tree-lined road heading towards Parliament Square not knowing, because of irregular signals, where any of his chasers were, and having no idea where Mike was on the long road wriggling and twisting behind him. But he was right there, staring hard at the number 1 on Read's back, looking for tell-tale signs of trouble from the big and hearty Honda.

The crowd lining the entrance to the right-hander into the square erupted, and gave Read the answer to the puzzle that had been troubling him for a while.

'To say I was surprised when he caught up with me,' said Phil, 'is putting it mildly. He came burbling up alongside me – but there was no nod from him. He was concentrating. And really hard, too. There was no tomfoolery right then. We both knew we had a job to do: a cat and mouse affair.'

Mike said: 'It was lovely to see him just ahead of me. I drifted by him, but he put on a bit of showbiz and outbraked me going into the big square. Just like Phil. But it was just what I expected him to do. I followed him through the section and uphill out of Ramsey towards the mountain. We passed and re-passed each other and I flapped my elbows about a bit as a little joke. We nodded to each other a couple of times, but mostly we got on with the racing.

'I wasn't too bothered about rubbing it in, or trying to get away from him too far. I knew that once I had caught him I was okay, provided Tommy Herron didn't pick up any more time.

'I honestly could not see anything stopping me winning – unless, naturally, there was some problem with the bike. But it was running perfectly; a dream in fact.'

Said Phil: 'I couldn't see anything to stop him, either. I could not have gone any quicker. That would have been impossible. I was right on my limit, I was going as fast as the machine would let me and there was nothing, not a mile an hour more, left. I decided the only way I could put a stop to Mike was to try and break the Ducati. 'So that's what I set about doing. But it was my bike that broke instead ...

'I had made up a little time back on him. And when we came into the pits for fuel I got away ahead of him – but there was no getting away *from* him. Within a few miles he had caught me again. He was a bloody nuisance; there was no shaking him off. And, remember, with the time difference I not only had to break clear I had to add to it and attempt to get back that lost 50 seconds. The way he was riding, with all his old flair and dash, it was a forlorn hope.

'I was in despair. He looked to me to be as good as he ever had been. And not even his obvious problems with braking and peel-off points made much difference. On the twisty bits he looked like the genius who had always haunted me.'

Phil made one last desperate bid to push Mike into an error of overtaxing the Ducati. He redlined the Honda, sent the tacho needle flickering way over the mark where it was safe to be and dragged a burst of speed and revs out of it that it was not designed to give. It was a move doomed to failure, the tactics of the desperate. And it failed. An oil seal blew and the Honda's lifeblood drained from it, rivulets of hope squirted from the heart of the engine. Blue smoke wisped from its innards and like clanking armour the big motor collapsed and died under Read's eager hands. Eleven miles of lap five had fled under the wheels of the two machines fronting the excitement for the spectators: Mike had refused to be lured into the trap Read was trying to set him.

'He was much too old a campaigner to fall for it, I suppose,' said Phil. 'He played it cool, did it his own way. He's done it so often before at the TT. And he knows how to ride a TT.

'That's important. And you never lose it once you've got it. It's not like any normal race where you are in direct competition with another man; you ride against the course and against time. And to do a TT as it should be done is a special knack. Mike has it. I have it, too. And that's why we made such a good race of it, even though on corrected time we were 50 seconds apart.'

The second lap, when Mike set his sights on Read's elusive tail and forced on to put some space between him and Herron, was completed by Mike at a speed of 110.25mph. Herron, with only one lap of his effort left, rounded the circuit at 109.55mph. Read did 108.37mph, Williams 107.06mph, Richards 106.85mph and new sixth-placed man, Alex George, lapped at 105.96mph.

Herron, who had closed to within four seconds of Mike at one stage, suddenly ran into trouble on lap three. He climbed off the ailing Honda, tried to put right the problems that had slowed it, but could not get back into the action. And, once he had gone, Mike was left more than 50 seconds ahead of Phil with lap four to come.

Mike, in complete control, hit a record high on the third lap, the halfway mark. He set a new lap record of 110.27mph. This on a road-going machine, fractions only less than the best times set on full-blooded, out-and-out race machinery. It really was a stirring, if crushing, show from the comeback man.

Read managed 108.74mph on fading ambition. Williams, as hopeful as ever, plugged away with 107.58mph. Scotsman Alex George, fourth, lapped at 106.09 – his great glory was to come a year later. In fifth place was Dahne, the man who had been mesmerised by Mike's style, at 105.97mph. Sixth, and seeing nothing of Mike since they had pushed off together, was Richards with a lap of 105.75. He was certainly feeling the pace, but he was hanging on.

The fourth lap saw little change. Mike, having seen Herron drop out and knowing full well he could contain Read, lapped at 108.85mph. Read did 107.79mph. Third placed Williams lapped at 106.34mph ahead of Richards's 106.14mph, Dahne at 105.07mph and Alex George slipping back on the Triumph into sixth place at 105.04mph.

After Read's fight back had collapsed on a bike that had become as useless as a clothes horse in the Grand National, and a heartbroken Herron had pulled out too, Mike underlined his authority with a slight upward surge that took him to 109.05mph on lap five.

Williams made it round at 106.66, more than two minutes adrift in second place, but two minutes in front of third man, Ian Richards who was lapping at 105.64mph. Dahne, as steady as ever, lapped at 105.56mph, George at 105.41mph and new leader-board challenger, Charlie Mortimer, at 103.77. But there was a gap of nearly five minutes from front to back of the scoreboard. There was no catching Mike ...

'And it was terrible in a way,' he said, 'everybody was waving to me, just as they had been from the very start. I'd never known that before – but when I started on the last lap I had my heart in my mouth all the way round.

'People were waving and jumping up and down, but I didn't return a single wave. I kept my hands on the grips, kept my concentration turned on and hoped against all hope that nothing would go wrong.

'It was by far the longest lap I've ever known at the TT. I couldn't wait for it to end. I could not bring myself to speed it up, or slow it down. I just kept on going at what I hoped was a normal sort of lick.

'As I got closer to the chequered flag the tears started to stream down my face. I was so full up with the emotion of it all, with the reaction I could see from the crowds lining the road and the cheers I could hear even over the noise of the engine, that I couldn't help myself. When I saw the finish line looming up I could not believe I had done it, in fact it didn't really hit me until about three weeks later.'

Two minutes behind him, wrestling with a petrol tank that had jumped loose from its moorings, John Williams was heading for second place. Ahead of him, 100 yards along the road, at the peel-off point to the winner's enclosure, I was jumping up and down like a man demented. Mike screeched the Ducati to a halt at my knees and we bear hugged in sheer delight at his win. He could not talk or he would have burst into a flood of tears. I could only repeat: 'Fantastic ... absolutely fantastic.'

He propped the bike up against the grey stone wall and hauled off the fly-spattered helmet. Sweat beaded his forehead; his eyes were red rimmed from the wind that had been whipping under an ill-fitting visor, and his head was pounding and raw where the helmet had rubbed and gnawed at his brow, threatening to wreck his concentration. It was virtually impossible to see anything through the mess of insects smeared across the visor-but he was happy.

We hugged like Cup Final teammates: I had made the pass, he had scored the winner. I have certainly never felt such a surge of inner satisfaction and well-being: Mike, I know, was the same. He gasped: 'I've had some wins, here and in the rest of the world, but for sheer emotion this beats them all. I can't explain how I feel. It's beyond all my dreams. Unbelievable.'

MIKE THE BIKE – AGAIN

The way into the winner's enclosure was parted for him; he was back on familiar territory. The crush of people, the monsoon of champagne and tangle of television wires and microphones, the gatling-like click-click of cameras, and smiles as far as the distant horizon, were the noisy, colourful recognition of his amazing feat.

It is there, under those circumstances, that an alter ego takes charge of Hailwood the rider, the absolute hero. He almost vanishes beneath a fog of shyness and only that which he feels is necessary, and not foolish, is done for the cameramen. Histrionics, the almost drunken, part-hysterical replies to questions, and silly poses are for somebody else. Instead, he recognises and waves to the distant face, the friend separated from the central figure by wave upon wave of strangers. You could be forgiven for thinking that somebody, a double, has pulled on his livery. That the man so daring, so sure, so confident, when he is astride a bucking, roaring motorcycle, edging and inching through spaces no wider than his shoulders at 170 miles-an-hour, is a twin. Same face – different personality.

The enclosure was a maelstrom; everybody, sponsors, officials and media men wanted a piece of the action, a chunk of the great man. But across a divide filled with faces and congratulations he saw me and made a dialling and telephone signal, mouthing 'Pauline'.

I raced back to where the 'phone was already linked with Pauline at her friend's home. 'He's done it!' I yelled – and just about everybody in the grandstand heard my shouts. Pauline burst into tears. And, just in front of me, climbing the steps up to the winner's dais was Mike, rubbing his eyes, fighting the tears, glancing over his shoulder at the scoreboard. Behind him was John Williams shouting: 'It's a pleasure to be beaten by a guy like that.' He had made it, after a brave bid, into second place. Ian Richards was third. He, too, was delighted to be sharing the same four square yards of planking as Mike.

John Williams had finished two minutes behind Mike: Ian Richards a further minute away from the winner. But it was no disgrace.

The final log was, Mike in 2hrs 5m 10.2s, an average speed of 108.51mph, a new record. Williams' time was 2hrs 7m 9.6s, with Richards third, in 2hrs 8m 7.4s. Fourth was Helmut Dahne in 2hrs 8m 26.8s, fifth was Alex George with 2hrs 8m 28.2s, and sixth was Charlie Mortimer in 2hrs 10m 50.4s.

John Williams, his face split with the widest smile imaginable, met up with Mike in a hospitality marquee behind the main grandstand. He told him: 'If I couldn't win it, and you didn't give me much of a chance once you'd got it all together, I wanted you to win it. You didn't disappoint me ... or anybody else, either. I thought you were unbelievable. I'll just have to make sure I get my own back later in the week.'

Back at the hotel Mike and I went straight into the bar for a quiet celebratory drink – vodka and lemonade for him, his first for nearly a fortnight, a brandy for me. We sat in the terrace window, overlooking the promenade, where thousands of enthusiasts who could not believe what they had just seen out there on the circuit, were making their way back to their hotels and boarding houses.

We sat opposite each other, drinks still on the table, and both just smiled the silly smiles of men who could not be happier, but who could not bring themselves to say anything. Then we laughed ... loud and long. And drank. And, indeed, drank a lot that night.

Mike went off to his top-floor bedroom to bathe away the stiffness of two hours and five minutes of racing on the world's most demanding circuit. He had spanned the treacherous gap of eleven years as if he had never been away at all. The years had rolled away to nothing. Natural talent had transcended all the pitfalls, had made a nonsense of doubt and had seen him safely through the most gruelling challenge that motorcycle road racing could offer.

When he answered a knock at his door he found Phil Read, still in his leathers, standing there. 'He came to offer his congratulations,' said Mike, 'and I thought that was really sporting of him. Phil must have felt terribly disappointed, but the old bugger came all the way back to my hotel to have a chat.'

'What else could I do?' said Phil, 'Mike's win, and his little Derby with me, was out of this world. I have enjoyed his victory as much as I enjoyed our dice. He deserves it, there was certainly nothing lucky about it. Even if I'd kept going there was no way I'd have got away from him.

'When we were racing so hard against each other I felt inspired. I honestly did. It was like the old days all over again. And I know the crowd loved every minute of it. I was using every bit of the road – Mike was only using half of it. I couldn't offer any more. I was at my limit; it would not have been physically possible for me to put any more effort into it.'

He added: 'I know what it's like coming back to the TT, I did it in 1977 after only a five-year lay-off. And it's extremely difficult. The mental pressure that builds up around you, not only before the race but very much during it, can be a real wrecker. You certainly feel it physically, too.'

He turned to Mike, who had been listening intently, without comment, and asked: 'How do you do it?'

Mike's reply: 'Dunno, mate. It must be something they put in the tea here.'

Any serious examination of his unique skill while he is around to hear it immediately sends Mike into his shell; he is as embarrassed by acclaim as he is angry with people who patronise him when he has failed to deliver, and they are looking for escape routes for him. And he cannot tell a lie. He is reluctant to be untruthful; a totally uncomplicated and straightforward character dwells happily under his skin. Nor does he enjoy asking for money which is due to him, even contract cash that he has signed for. If it is not delivered to him unsolicited he refuses steadfastly to go looking or asking for it – and it does not matter what the figure is. There were a good few reluctant or slow payers after both the 1978 and

MIKE THE BIKE – AGAIN

1979 TTs, and one company, a big firm but with the smallest outlay of all involved, who still had not paid up their 1978 debt by the start of 1980 – nor will they ever. And there is no way that Mike will demand it.

If the speed at which riders like Mike deliver their end of any bargain were matched by the finalisation of the deal from the sponsor's side there would be a much happier atmosphere in racing – and a few more riders off the breadline.

None of this clouded Mike's mind as we set out for a party in a restaurant that had been taken over by Sports Motorcycles: the place was jammed, the pianola squeaking *There'll Always Be an England*, and champagne being swigged from pint pots. In a corner sat three Italians, all Ducati experts sent over by the Bologna-based factory. One of them could only sit and mutter: 'Fantastic! Ducati, world champion. Fantastic!' And when a wild tug-o'-war, from the cafe into the street, started up at 2am he sat in the melee, still sober, still intoning 'Ducati, world champion.' And every time Mike passed him he had to shake his hand. He was shell-shocked by the whole magnificent affair, by a day that had reduced him to tears of happiness, by a man he considered to be a god riding a machine he had helped to develop and then set up for the race – and by one of the most memorable achievements in Ducati's history.

There were a lot of bad heads the next morning, a lot of leftover joy, too. For what had seemed impossible had turned into glorious reality and the doubters had been forced to eat their words. One man in particular, puffed up with his own importance, who had suggested that he had turned Mike down for a ride – incidentally, without being approached – must have hoped for the earth to open up.

Mike and I breakfasted together to discuss the possibilities for the next day's Senior race, the 500cc event in which he was to ride Giacomo Agostini's ex-Grand Prix machine. And he revealed: 'If I hadn't agreed and contracted to do the rest of the week I'd have packed up altogether after yesterday's win. After that, what else is there?

'Unfortunately, I'm committed and I won't go back on my arrangements, but I wish I could stop ... right here and now. I'm not looking forward one bit to what's left of the week. I'd much rather retire and get boozed up every night.

'The Formula One win was so easy for me, no problem at all. I just trundled round; I never revved it more than 8,500 at any stage. I know I could have gone very much quicker, even though my braking was awful, probably up to 112mph – but there was no need. It was good to have so much in hand, and once Phil and Tom had dropped out my worries were over. Unless, of course, the engine had gone sick on me. But I know full well it's not going to be so easy for the rest of the racing. The 500, for instance, I've only done four practice laps on it and it's so different from the four-strokes I've got used to that I'll have to learn to ride it while I'm racing.

'And that 750 ... well ... what can I say about that. It still terrifies me. Man wasn't meant to go that fast. I know I'll just never get the hang of it and the best I can hope for is probably to get onto the leader board. Even that would be something of an achievement, and it doesn't thrill me at all. And I suppose the nearer I get to Friday when I've got to race it, the less sleep I'll get. I wonder if we can arrange to get it pinched from the lock-up ...'

At the garage the three Yamaha mechanics were rehearsing the petrol quick-filler action – something like seven gallons flooding into the tank in seven seconds from a hand-held container. They had got it down to a fine art when Mike joined them in practice in the narrow lane that ran beside the hotel where the lock-up was situated. Vital seconds were being played for; the difference between joyous victory or sad defeat. And the plan of action for the halfway mark, three lap refuel stop, was as essential to get right as the setting for the carburettors. There was little else to do except the last-minute checks – and, later that night, when the mechanics were doing just that Mike called to see them ...

He would have done better to stay away. But, as he always did when he was Grand Prix racing, he liked to let the hard-working mechanics see that the star was not beyond their reach and was as much involved behind the scenes as they were in their anonymous labours.

The bike looked magnificent, it WAS magnificent. And the Martini colour scheme gave it a sweet, racy look. There were no problems reported by the mechanics, not since Nobby Clarke, lifting the machine into the van after Friday practice, two days before, had noticed the front end sink dramatically when he braked it. And then the rear stay stiff as he backed it: he had discovered that the frame had broken ...

Frame expert Ken Sprayson had put matters right and the 500 was just about as ready as Nobby, Tilbury and Jerry Wood could get it. Mike, having left his dinner to walk the 100 yards from his hotel to the garage to see the Yamaha team, let his eyes roam over the machine. A thought struck him; the 750, he felt, had handled better than the 500 and he put it down to the damping.

He was hesitant about giving the mechanics any more to do, but he thought it would be a good idea to switch the damper from the big bike onto the 500. 'I'm sure it'll improve things,' he pointed out, 'so would you make the alteration?' It had not occurred to him then, nor did it until a year later, that the handling problems he had suffered with the 500 might have been due entirely to the split frame. But, in any case, there was no way he could find out. There was no time left. And the spannermen did his bidding – they swapped the Kawasaki damper, one that could be modified as he raced, from the superbike onto the Senior machine. It proved to be just about the most costly idea Mike had ever had at the TT – and, anyway, by the time he had returned to our hotel his dinner had gone cold.

He was in bed by 10.30pm, nicely keyed up about the Senior race, the event he had almost made his own over the years, but, once again, he slept fitfully. This time, unlike previous years, he did not resort to sleeping tablets. The 500, he felt, was a pleasant enough machine and most certainly good enough to beat anything else in the race.

'The power comes in at about 8,500 revs,' he explained, 'and then ... WOW! ... you know you are on your way. But it's a super little bike and I'm sure that when I get used to it, when I've got the hang of it and can ride it as it should be ridden, then I'll enjoy myself. At the moment, with only four practice laps on it, it's an entirely new entity to me. And there's no way I can race it like I raced the Ducati on Saturday in the Formula One – I'll be looking for different lines, different braking and peel-off points. I'll just have to feel my way round for a lap or so, hope I've got it right and then, if I can, if I'm in contention, have a real go.'

He was fourth fastest in practice. American Pat Hennen, Barry Sheene's teammate in the Suzuki-GB World 500cc Championship team, who was to be so tragically injured in a crash at 165 miles-an-hour on the last lap of the race, topped the leaderboard of practice times. He had gone round in 20m 19.4s, a speed of 111.38mph. Second fastest was Herron, killed a year later in his native Ulster, with a lap of 111.13mph. Cheshire man Stan Woods was third fastest at 108.73mph with Mike, fourth, at 107.57mph.

Next came Scotsman Alex George, the former Manx Grand Prix winner, who had lapped at 107.56mph, and then Charlie Williams, another Cheshire man, with a lap of 107.16mph set up on a 350cc Yamaha.

If anybody had any doubts about Hennen's pace, or thought it might have been a flash in the pan from the comparative newcomer to TT racing, he wiped them all out with the most breathtaking lap of all in training for the Classic, the race for superbikes to be staged on the last day, Friday.

He became the first man ever to lap the fearsome 37¾ miles, over the mountain and down again, around the walking-pace Ramsey hairpin and the slow twists into the start-and-finish straight, in less than 20 minutes. He went round in 19m 54s – a staggering lap at 113.75mph, and a phenomenal individual performance. What was even more remarkable was his reaction to the news, though whether his gamesmanship was in full flood at the time I'm not sure. For he said: 'Really, as fast as that? I honestly wasn't hardly trying; I was well within myself and not hurrying anywhere, not sticking my neck out at all.'

There was much headshaking and I for one feared that Pat, as great a Grand Prix and short circuit competitor as he had developed into, was treading a quicksand at the TT. This, I would like to stress, is not wisdom after the event. I voiced my opinion, suggested that his caution had evaporated a little too much, that his eagerness to do well may have overridden his own sensibly adjusted safety margins from the year before. But he merely broke into that winning grin of his and answered: 'Nope, not at all. I'm taking it easy. It's just that it's all going together for me. And I feel real good.'

Whatever, he went into the Senior TT, pace fused to confidence, with the armour-plating of being the fastest man on the island. There were some extremely fine riders who would have loved to have earned that accolade – but, I'm certain, they would rather say they had just done that speed and not that they were going to try to do it in an hour's time. Mike, no doubt looking forward to the Classic, the race Hennen was destined to miss, summed up most men's feelings when he considered Pat's relative inexperience at the TT, and matched it with his speed. 'He's welcome to it,' he said, 'and there's no way I'm going to try and get round here at that pace.

'Not with all the money I've got in the bank.'

Hennen's mood, however, was buoyant. He was, he felt, in complete control and, before his high-speed appointment with the Senior, he promised 'I'll be trying 85 per cent of my ability and that leaves plenty of room, and road, for safety purposes. It's not my own judgement that gives me any cause for anxiety, it's the worry about mechanical failure on a circuit where you don't get too many second chances. I've built into my racing at the TT a wide margin to cope with the unexpected; it's the only way to race here.'

Mike, the focus of everybody's attention, did not relish having to go as fast as his supporters wanted him to. The aftermath of his fairy tale victory in the Formula One had taken its toll, and his mood did not give him the hungry edge he'd had before the F1 chase. He was not casual or uncaring – he would just rather have stayed in bed, but with that awful self-punishing sense of responsibility he suffers, he had to jazz himself up for the effort.

'A place on the leaderboard will do for me,' he said. 'But we'll see what happens when we get going.'

7
Senior drama

Mike was talking, swinging the wheel of the car and smoothing out the bends on the way up to the circuit: 'Things have gone well so far ... too well, really. Makes you wonder, doesn't it?'

His leather livery had changed; the red, white and gold of the Formula One had given way to sleeker black leathers, banded around the middle with the name and colour of Martini.

His friend and honorary team member, Dickie Attwood, the former Grand Prix race car driver and Le Mans 24-hour expert, had wobbled off on a big Yamaha, blackboard under his arm and a pocketful of chalk, towards Ramsey to set up a signalling station. It did not matter to the ever-cheerful Attwood that motor bikes, and riding them, were not his forte; it was not entirely clear to us whether he had ever ridden one at all when he climbed aboard Mike's 1100cc superbike and pointed it towards Ramsey. His view was that it was bound to have a throttle, a clutch and brakes and, therefore, it was similar to a car, and must be simplicity itself to ride.

It was a philosophy we did not share too readily – but he seemed content and his infectious enthusiasm just to be involved in the operation blinded him to any attendant problems ... like how to ride a motor bike.

Mike was relaxed. The pre-race furore about quick-fillers, those hand-held petrol containers that jetted in fuel at a startling rate and wiped out the wastage of precious seconds, had ebbed quietly into the background. A furious Tom Herron, backed by an equally concerned Pat Hennen, had said that if there was any trouble about the fillers, a necessary adjunct to racing at such a high level, then, in the Irishman's words: 'They can stick their race.'

We decided to keep a low profile in the arguments and hid our filler under a blanket in the pits, the case to be argued with the officials after the event. But, fortunately, they saw the good sense in the fillers, the need for them, and though it was left for the duty fire officer to sort out, it never came to pass that the matter reached any sort of level as an issue.

Things *were* going too well. We set up our own signalling arrangement from the press box, where I had a phone, to the mechanics at the pit counter thirty yards or so away, but separated by a barrier of fencing.

Paul Butler, the Yamaha projects chief in Amsterdam, had another huge blackboard which, when necessary, was held up for Nobby Clarke to see and to act upon according to what messages we were getting from our points around the course. We had a phone in a garage in Ramsey – Attwood's responsibility – and one in a house at the spectacular Ballaugh Bridge. The massive back-up of sponsorship had grown up behind us in the grandstand area; the Martini marquee, its superb cuisine and endless drinks, dominated the scene. The famous drinks company had brought a new, smooth dimension to the sport and it was an exciting breakthrough. Unfortunately the clockwork ease with which their operation progressed was not matched by the affair they had come to support, but that was nobody's fault ...

Pat Hennen, John Williams and Tom Herron all pushed their Suzukis off the line, dropped clutches, blipped throttles, and uttered unheard sighs as their machines fired cleanly, picked up and sped away. Mike, number 12, coolly waited his turn to go, resting the Yamaha at his right hip, both hands on the grips and, unblinkingly, waited for the starter's flag to signal him to start. The cheers welled up from the grandstand as Mike wrestled the machine forwards. But it would not fire; he sweated and swore, put his shoulders behind compression as the cheers faltered and turned into groans. In the meantime the three Suzuki men were widening the gap between themselves and the wheezing Yamaha that had suffered some sort of mechanical asthma. After an eternity, with Nobby Clarke getting ready to sprint in like a relay man with a new plug as baton, the machine's weedy splutter turned into an echoing crackle, a clarion call to Hailwood's skill to make up the seconds he had lost, and he headed off towards the scattered showers of the mountain and the men who were already well on their way.

In Ramsey, poised to spring like a pantomime villain from his trapdoor, waited Attwood. He was almost lost in the crowd in and around Parliament Square and when Mike came swinging through, looking for some information, Dickie's blackboard might as well have been transparent. Mike did not see it, so he got his head down and just determined to go as fast as he could to make up the leeway he knew he had lost after that appalling start. He flew by the pits, wide on the road, soaking up Bill Smith and Charlie Williams as he went through, and, despite his horrible setback, was in fourth place. He had managed a lap of 108.54mph – 20m 51.14s – even with the handicap of the spluttering start to overcome. Up front Tom Herron was ahead of John Williams, with Hennen in third place. Tom had lapped at 110.62mph, John at 109.84mph and Pat at 109.18. It was obviously going to be a tremendous struggle and Mike was disappointed that he could not get within reach of them to hot things up even more.

Whatever chance he may have given himself was sabotaged by his own idea of the night before ... when he ordered Nobby Clarke to change the damper.

MIKE THE BIKE – AGAIN

Mike, having satisfactorily scrubbed in new tyres, pressed on a little harder and halfway round the second lap pulled into third place, only 8 seconds behind Hennen. The fireworks, it seemed, were about to begin ...

My 'phone rang. It was Attwood. 'Mike's in trouble – and I've been arrested!' Mike had had the life scared out of him with a huge wobble that he corrected only for it to happen again, leaving him less than happy with his lot.

He swept into Ramsey's Parliament Square looking for Dickie, drew to a halt by the roadside as the rest of the field roared by and yelled: 'The damper's broken. The bike's almost unridable. Tell Nobby I'm coming in and tell him I want it fixing.' That's when Dickie's enthusiasm got the better of him. He jumped into the road behind the Yamaha and gave it a shove to help Mike on his way ... a cardinal sin. The policeman moved quickly and scribbled the Attwood name into his pocket book, promising further action and banning him from his position, despite Dickie's explanations ...

Mike, unable to ride the machine any faster than 40 miles an hour, struggled with it for the 17 miles or so to the pits: I had told Nobby he was coming but he feared there was nothing that could be done. Mike pulled in, his face under the helmet a mask of dejection. The withering interest he'd had before the race had been replaced with a gritty determination to do his best – he could have quit right there and nobody would have been any the wiser. Certainly nobody would have complained, but that would not have been the dutiful, honest action in Mike's eyes. He sat astride the stilled Yamaha as Nobby hurried to solve the problem. A bush had pulled out of one end of the damper. Nobby unscrewed it, pushed on a large washer to hold in the bush and slapped Mike on the back to send him on his way again. But he had lost more than two minute – and not even a rider of Mike's calibre, even fired with the same keenness, could wipe out that sort of handicap in the pursuit of men like Herron, Hennen and Williams.

And that, really, was where it all ended for Mike in the Senior, the race he had won five times before in his TT career.

Pat Hennen crashed so badly on the last lap he was in a coma for months: John Williams, who died a year later in Ireland, dropped out of the chase with a broken radiator hose. And that left Herron to clinch it with a new race record of 111.74mph, five minutes ahead of second man Billy Guthrie, with Charlie Mortimer third.

Mike, too far back to make any impression on the front runners, was determined to keep going throughout the six laps. He struggled along with further trouble from the clutch until he ran out of petrol, borrowed some from a motorist parked by the roadside, and made it home into 28th place at an average of 99.36mph. His time for the 226 miles race was 2hrs 16m 41.8s. Herron's was 2hrs 0lm 33.4s. But tucked away in the comparative anonymity of the also-rans Mike managed to get round lap five at a speed of more than 112mph, his quickest ever race speed at the TT.

The reception for him at the prize presentation that night, when he collected his Formula One Trophy and his replica for 28th place in the Senior, was unforgettable. He was cool enough in the absolute bedlam of the evening to dedicate his big win to his father, Stanley, who had died earlier in the year. It was a night, he admitted, he would always remember, always treasure. And when we could not find a taxi to take us back to our hotel we skipped and ran down the promenade, giggling all the way, drunk as newts on the sheer pleasure and satisfaction of it all.

Attwood had returned the Yamaha in one piece; the policeman, no doubt having mentioned the triumph of his action to higher authority, had returned to the signalling post to say that, all considered, he had decided to take no further action. So the gallows, we told Dickie, would stay in store – though who they might have been used on I would not like to say.

We were two races down ... two to go. And by the day the euphoria was increasing like a fever. Nearly 400 newsmen were on the island – and, at some time or another, every one of them must have called at our hotel to talk to or photograph Mike.

There were dinners and lunches to attend, sponsors' trips, autographing sessions, interviews, photo calls, prizes to accept, places to go, friends to meet, shows to open, team conferences, parties to attend and so many kind people to thank personally that Mike's non-race days were a blur of activity. There was no escape from it all. And, as Mike said, it was a relief to get out and race because it was the only peace he got. Though he would not have held the same view had he been able to look into the future, at the outcome of the 250cc race and the final race of the week, the Classic ...

'Too bloody right,' he said, more than a little pained by the memory. 'Both of those races were disasters and the sooner I can forget about them the happier I'll be.

'The 250 race was bad enough – but the Classic just about shattered all my dreams. Worse still, it left me terribly embarrassed and extremely sorry for all the people who had made the journey to the Isle of Man especially to see me. I know there were a lot of people who had done just that.

'It was a nightmare for me. In fact, after the Formula One, the entire week turned into something highly forgettable. First, I couldn't get the 500 started in the Senior. I think I was opening the throttle too wide and it just wouldn't light up. I thought the way I was going I was going to have to run all the way round the course. I seemed to be pushing for ages before it started. There's a knack to starting these things and I just don't have it. Talk about being embarrassed ... I knew everybody was looking at me and that made me worse.

'Then, two days later, the 250. Disaster. Total disaster! I knew I had no chance on it, lovely little bike that it was, but I've never been entirely at home on the little ones. This one was no exception: I'd had trouble trying to start it before the race and Trevor Tilbury had fiddled about raising the needles to make it easier for me. I got it going okay, but that's all. I had hardly any idea at all how to ride it or do it justice. I'd only done two practice laps on it – and had fallen off. So me and the 250 were pretty much strangers to each other.

'By the time the 250 race came round I had my eyes cast a bit farther forward ... to the Classic and my tangle with Mick Grant. That, I'll admit, was topmost in my mind and I had decided to use the 250 as a bit of practice for the bigger race.

'By the time I got going, having looked around me at all those lightweight specialists, I settled down just to enjoy myself. And, to a great degree, I suppose I did. There was no real pressure on me, not like there was when I was out on the biggies, and after a lap or two I seemed to get the hang of the thing a bit more. Once I'd done that, and once I'd had a few of the chaps come by me, I got going some. Trevor had put together a nice motor, it must have been just about the quickest in the race and, in the end, I knocked up the second or third fastest lap of the race.

'There had been a bit of blunder on the size of our fuel tank; we should have had a bigger one but it seemed nobody had worked that out and I had to stop twice whereas the others were blazing round stopping only once for gas. After that I had no chance at all and I crept home in 12th place.'

The Classic, the confrontation between Mike and Mick Grant, the race the whole island had been looking forward to was to be the stage for the fastest, most ferocious dice of the entire week. But it flopped as the 750 superbike that Mike had forced himself to try to tame clattered and died under him as he drew dead level with race favourite Grant, the fastest man ever over the TT course.

The first lap fade-out left Grant saying later: 'I felt cheated when Mike went out. You know, the question you always ask yourself ... I wonder, could I have beaten him? Now I'll never know. After he had gone there was, I felt, nobody else to worry about. And it was the easiest money I've earned for a long time.

'But I'm sure he was just as disappointed as me. I know he would have set me up as a target; he knew I was good at the TT and, I'm certain, he was curious to see just how good I was. If I was better than him. But now it's all so much conjecture. But for me the Classic was devalued right there and then, the second I found out he'd not made it. I know it would have been one hell of a race and, though I don't like talking figures, I'm sure it would have been in the 115s.'

Mike countered: 'Those sort of speeds wouldn't have been out of my reach. I had always told myself that to beat Grant in a good race it would be necessary to be up there in the 115s. Whether I could have beaten him or not, I don't know. And there was no way I was going to kill myself trying, but it would have been an interesting episode.

'I really wanted to sign off the week with a big win. After the Formula One success, and the failures that followed, I'd set myself the Classic as the target. If I'd won it, or even if I'd done well and finished within sight of Mick, I am sure I would have retired from TT racing. As it was I felt the disappointment so much I decided as I sat in the hotel after the race to come back in 1979. I knew how disappointed the fans must have been. I felt for them. So many of them had travelled over especially on the Friday to see a race and what they got was a high-speed exhibition from Mick. A very fine, very fast rider, but still a race would have been more to their liking.'

Grant, of course, won at a canter. Despite a hanging rear brake caliper that could have meant disqualification, he streaked straight through a scheduled fuel stop on the fifth lap of the six-lap race to romp home at an average of 112.40mph; he had covered the 226 miles in 2hrs 0m 50.2s. He also lapped at a new record speed of 114.33mph. John Williams was second at 111.62mph for the six laps, and Alex George third at 109.39mph.

Mike was so downcast back at the hotel that we came the closest we have ever been to having an argument; I wanted him to snap out of it. His overdeveloped sense of loyalty and responsibility would not allow it.

'I feel as upset as I did when I lost the world title in Monza eleven years ago ... when the gearbox on the Honda broke up,' he told me. I certainly had not seen him as dejected since then – we had driven from Monza's Autodromo in total silence and it had stayed that way for nearly an hour.

'Okay,' I said, 'stay miserable until ...' and I looked at my watch '... say, seven o'clock. An hour. Then we'll get stoned.'

When we met in the bar an hour later it was as if somebody had waved a wand over him; he looked back to his unbelievable Formula One victory, savoured the success of it, and we set about demolishing the contents of the famous Round Bar. But three hours later he slipped quietly away from the dinner table and walked through the milling crowds along the seafront to the hotel where the Yamaha mechanics were staying and working. He found them, still oily and weary, poring over the jigsaw of metal that was the 750 engine, performing the post-mortem. It was midnight before they came up with the answer: the crankshaft had broken. There was not a thing they, or Mike, could have done to alter that.

In a nearby nightclub Mike found out that he had been voted 'Man of the Week' by a panel of journalists. But he gave the trophy to Mick Grant – even if he did keep the cheque that went with it ...

I next saw him queueing for a cup of tea at Ronaldsway Airport, waiting for his flight back to England. He was on his way to Mallory Park, where, against all the odds but underlining his undimmed genius, he won. He attacked from the back of the field, finished with his feet bleeding out of a gaping gash in his boots, and steamrollered his way to an amazing win as 30,000 ecstatic, disbelieving spectators watched in awe.

I could not go. I had lost my voice; but he telephoned me that night, made light of his win saying that the youngsters these days did not have the fight they should, and said: 'What about the TT next year? Wanna do it again?'

8

Here we go again

I had vowed that nothing would induce me to go through the stage management of another Hailwood appearance at the TT; it was, I felt, like trying to organise an epic. The wear and tear on the nerves and the severe testing of one's patience, allied to the day-to-day organisation of the most wanted man in the motorcycle world for a fortnight, was almost too much to suffer. But the sheer joy of sharing the ultimate reward of victory, of knowing you had a part in it and were the link between the great man and the world that revolved around him, was in its own way a sucker punch. I knew full well the consequences of going through it all for a second time, but I jutted my chin and plunged in with my eyes wide open; it was another knock-out year ...

When the North Sea ferry Norland slipped her moorings at Hull, on England's eastern seaboard, and nosed her great bulk towards Rotterdam taking me on the first steps to Holland for the Dutch TT, a fortnight after the heady experiences of the Isle of Man, I had a briefcase jammed with offers for Mike.

There had been no escape before the ramp of the ferry and its comfortable innards; my letter-box at home had been regularly fed with mail from all over the world, and the telephone had never stopped ringing. Now I had eighteen hours of wonderful peace to look forward to, a gentle cruise through the late afternoon and the night, and I could see the Yorkshire coastline getting fainter in the wispy mist. I was part way through dinner, enjoying the glow of the claret, when the Norland's tannoy called me for a ship-to-shore phone link call. It was an Italian, asking me to persuade Mike to race at a meeting where the appearance money would be phenomenal, much more than he had ever earned, even in his heyday. There was no escape. Not for me. Not for Mike. Though later he cleared off home to New Zealand saying, almost over his shoulder: 'Next year I'll be coming back to England to stay. But let's get the TT organised; I want to make up for my let-down of all those people who came to see me and missed out.' No amount of arguing that he had nothing to prove, that he had, indeed, pleased everybody could dissuade him from his view.

The Dutch TT organisers wanted Mike to race in their 500cc world championship round, and though he was flattered by the offer, considerable by anybody's standards, he turned them down. The 130,000 fans who annually watch the racing on the circuit at Assen, in the north of the country, do not realise just how hard the organisers strove to persuade Mike. It was precisely the same with all the big money internationals, the non-championship events that draw huge crowds and pay immense amounts of money to the top stars ... £7000-£10000 in some cases. And if ever there was a year that Mike could have cashed in, probably earning three or four times more than he had during his last, and probably finest, year in Grand Prix racing in 1967, it was in 1978. But he said: 'I'm not in it for the money.' And it was one hell of a job to get the point across to men who were used to hearing their money speak loud and clear in a sport where cash is king, and often god.

Kenny Roberts was on his way to his first world 500cc title in his debut year of Grand Prix racing – but he could not push the name of Hailwood off the front pages of the magazines. I followed the battle between Barry Sheene and Roberts to West Germany, to the Nürburgring in fact, a place of sad memory because of its near destruction of Mike in that horrendous Formula One car crash in 1974.

And after Kenny had clinched his title on a cool August afternoon in 1978 and was celebrating in that wonderfully noisy, infectious way he has, I opened negotiations with Yamaha's top brass for machinery for Mike for the 1979 TT. We talked earnestly at one end of the bar in the hotel attached to the circuit, while at the other end Kenny drank anything that anybody pushed into his very talented hands. Nobody in the place realised what was going on only a few feet away from the heart of the party. But I felt the Japanese were still smarting somewhat at the failure of their equipment in the Isle of Man, because when I asked for a 500 – maybe even Kenny's title winner – the answer was fogged with regret.

'I regret I cannot let you have a 500cc machine,' said the high-ranking Japanese, the man with the power of veto. 'We feel we would not have a machine that would adequately meet Mr Hailwood's very fine reputation. And unless we could provide him with a machine that would equal his standing as one of the finest riders of all time then we would rather not lend him a machine at all.

'We will not have enough 1979 500s to lend him a new one, and we feel that an old one would not be up to his standard of requirement. He can, if he wishes, be provided with a 750 and a 250 but, regrettably, no 500. I am sorry.'

No amount of persuasion would entice him to change his mind; we felt that even the old Agostini 500 would be good enough. But that was already on its way back to Japan and there was no way the Yamaha hierarchy wanted to risk being outpaced in a race that received as much publicity as the TT, and especially with Hailwood on its machine.

I followed up my verbal requests with a letter, but not even the chance of huge publicity returns would alter their view.

For seven months I chased after a Yamaha 500: even from Daytona, at the American classic, I made a 4am call to the factory to speak to another high-ranker. But after another let-down I had to give best to their convictions and look elsewhere ...

The all-conquering Ducati was, of course, already pencilled into our plans. The Auto-Cycle Union, once again through Vernon Cooper, had agreed fully to our requirements and it only remained to fix up a 500cc machine that would give Mike the ride his talent demanded. The answer to the problem was obvious. There was only one machine to satisfy that need – the Suzuki.

Suzuki-GB, always eager to reap the benefits of publicity, had asked me tentatively after the 1978 TT if Mike might join their Grand Prix set-up. With that brand of go-ahead thinking they did not ponder too long when I approached them to provide one of their super-fast 500s for the 1979 TT.

Maurice Knight, the Suzuki-GB chief, took up team manager Rex White's recommendations and contacted the factory in Japan. The answer was swift: 'Sign Hailwood. We'll give you all the support you require.'

Where Yamaha had been reluctant to tread Suzuki, their big business rivals who, in 1978 after the TT, replaced them as second largest sellers in the United Kingdom, eagerly rushed in. They offered one of their incredibly fast superbikes, too – but we turned that one down. Mike's view was that it was just too quick for sensible island racing.

Barry Sheene's chief mechanic, Martin Ogborne, the brains behind his world championship engines, was told that he would be working for Mike at the TT. He said: 'I can't believe it. Working for God! Me. That's fantastic. I just hope I can get everything okay for him.' In fact, Ogborne was a bag of nerves until he met up with Mike, his boyhood idol, at a test session ...

He had half a season of Grand Prix racing to cover before he flew to the island for the link-up with Mike. He said: 'I couldn't wait, the weeks seemed to drag by until I got off that 'plane at Ronaldsway. It was a life's ambition to mechanic for the man.' He, David Cullen and Gordon Whitehead were to work under Rex White's guidance, a complete Grand Prix back-up, at the TT.

Mike flew in from New Zealand via California where he, Pauline, and their two children had snatched a holiday, then almost immediately set off for Misano, Italy, for a test session on what should have been the brand new and improved Ducatis. Pat Slinn, from Sports Motorcycles went, too, and so did Vince French, the Champion spark plug expert. But behind the scenes at the Bologna factory there had been all manner of problems; the machines were not what they should have been, there were money difficulties, and it looked as if Sports Motorcycles, the little Manchester independents matched against the multi-nationals, would have to foot the massive bills.

To this background, Mike set about putting the big twin through its paces – and it nearly cost him his life. The machines had not even been tested and, worse, the gearbox was the wrong way round from that which Mike had used at the previous TT. It could scarcely be described as a replica, for even the most casual approach should have guaranteed a gear-shift that was a copy of the one on the machine that had won the world Formula One championship.

But the machines were a disaster. Mike, always ready to accept that he may be at fault, thought that he was race rusty and not doing the machine justice when he thundered it around Misano – but, plainly, the 15bhp extra that had been promised by the Italians was not there. The bike was not nearly so fast as it had been a year before, and this was the one which they claimed had been vastly improved.

'Then, of course, I got pitched off,' said Mike. 'And it nearly killed me. It was the worst crash of my life and I was so lucky to get away with only a couple of fractured ribs and a good deal of bruising.

'I went into a corner in neutral at about 70 or 80 miles-an-hour and changed down instead of up – the gearbox was upside down from what I'd been used to – and it was like hitting a wall. The back wheel locked up, the bike slid sideways, suddenly gripped and threw me over the top. Highsiding, they call it. I was flung off like a rag doll.

'In previous crashes I'd had some semblance of control over my body – but not this time. I'd never been hurled right over the top before. I had no chance to ball myself up or take any emergency action; my arms and legs and head were flailing about all over the place and then the bike clouted me. I've never been in such pain in my life, it was terrible.

'I was convinced I wouldn't get out of it alive. When I found I was still breathing my first thought was to get home as quickly as I could. Vince French squeezed me into his little hire car and we motored back to Milan – it seemed a thousand miles to me – to catch a 'plane back to London. When I got to Linate airport I'd seized, I could hardly get out of the car. And the plane trip ... that was just awful. Every bump, every air pocket was sheer agony.

'When I got to Heathrow I couldn't go a step further; I just booked into the nearest hotel and collapsed in bed for the night. I went to hospital the next day and they told me I'd done my ribs in. It was ages before I felt right again. I don't recommend anybody to break their ribs.'

The biggest hurt of all was that Ducati, who had feted him so gratefully the year before, had faltered so badly in their support and, apparently, their interest. The machine was a pale shadow of the thoroughbred it had been at the 1978 TT and, it seemed to me, they were happy to let Mike make up for its deficiencies with his usual response of gritty effort. It was not good enough – but we were not to know just how bad it was until the factory sent the race machines to England to be set up for the island's rigours.

'I couldn't believe it. The bikes were terrible,' said Mike. 'They were not a patch on the '78 machines. And the handling! It was dreadful. I thought it must be me and I was glad when Eddie Roberts and George Fogarty, the other two lads in the team, had a go and had the same feeling.

'The frames were brand new, so were the front forks and other bits and pieces. But instead of improving the bikes they had progressed backwards very quickly. I don't know how many times the settings were changed – hundreds, but it made no difference.'

It was totally mystifying. Ducati sent two men across with the bikes and even though they and the Sports Motorcycles guys got their heads together it was impossible to find the answer to the handling difficulties. Behind all this, of course, was the problem, too, of decreased power. We were defeated, short of fresh ideas and unable to get things right, or even nearly right. In the end, after sessions at Donington Park and Oulton Park, and after every possible permutation of change, we decided to leave it to the Isle of Man and try to iron out the handling there.

'The Suzuki was another thing altogether. It was beautiful. And I could not have been happier with it. After only four laps on it, the first time I'd ridden it, I told the lads to leave it alone. I thought it was marvellous.

'I'd heard so many bad reports about the thing and had seen Tommy Herron and Barry Sheene after they'd fallen off them at the Spanish Grand Prix, just before the TT, that I was scared to death of them. Tommy and Barry didn't have too much that was good to say about them, and just about every rider I spoke to warned me to be ultra-careful.

'I met Tommy and Barry at Heathrow airport and they tottered off the 'plane, both of them bandaged and looking distinctly grey, and I wondered what the hell I might be letting myself in for. I'd already seen Barry on television when, somehow, he got out of a spectacular slide at Brands Hatch. That put me off, too.

'But as soon as I got on it I felt at home and in no time at all at Donington I was getting round in very respectable times, not too short of the lap record.'

Chief mechanic Martin Ogborne, watching from the trackside and timing Mike as he rounded Donington Park's hilly acres, said: 'We've set the machine up as near as we can for the TT. I've kept all my records from the island in a little book and I knew exactly what to do to get it reasonably right for the TT.'

When Mike coasted back to the pits he was smiling widely. He lifted his visor and said to Martin: 'Great, just great. I like it very much indeed, and power ... jeez ... there's tons of it.'

Added Ogborne: 'I could hardly believe what I was hearing. Nothing wrong with it! It was so unusual not to have some sort of criticism. But Mike is in a class of his own. Other men would have found something wrong just to get you geed up. Not Mike! And I didn't know what to do with myself. I'd expected to be working for the rest of the day – and was prepared to. But no! Mike told us to shove the bike in the van, lengthen the gear lever for his gammy foot and fetch it to the Isle of Man.

'Oh, there was one thing wrong. The paint job. It was to be sprayed in his own red, white and gold livery and it hadn't been done exactly as he wanted it. And that was it! I had another look under his helmet to make sure it was him – and then packed up to go back to Suzuki headquarters at Croydon. It was as easy as that.'

If only it had been as simple with the Ducati – but that was a handful of difficulties and discrepancies, and they became no easier as the TT drew closer, whatever backbreaking, all-night effort Steve Wynne and Pat Slinn put into it.

'Everything else went perfectly smoothly, absolutely as we wanted,' said Mike. 'There were no problems. We had got a good team together with Suzuki, the back-up was just as I wanted, and I knew that if I didn't win the Senior, at least, and put up a good show in the Classic, then I should get my backside kicked.

'We had no problems with sponsorship that had gone according to plan. Ted offered Martini the chance to come in again as overall sponsor, and a couple of other big companies, too, but they opted out. In the end he suggested it would be an idea to paint the Suzuki in my own colours as I was going to go into business with Rod Gould right after the '79 TT – and we could use it as an advertising hoarding for Hailwood and Gould. And that's what we did.

'But the Duke ... that was an increasing problem. And it didn't take me too long to work out that, whereas Honda had progressed in giant strides, Ducati had gone backwards with even bigger ones. The gulf between the two was enormous. I felt it even before we got going on the island – and once we were there all my fears were found to be true. Though, I must stress, it was certainly no fault of Sports Motorcycles – they'd invested a fortune in the effort.'

After the lessons of 1978, when Mike could find no haven of quiet, I had arranged for him to have a hideaway house on the outskirts of Douglas, between the town and the TT track. It was the perfect answer. He still had a room in the town's Palace Hotel for practice week – it was not so bad then – but when race week proper started he moved up to the house on the hill. There, he could play the piano, entertain friends and, most important of all, relax away from the pressures of popularity that were, paradoxically, a penalty.

There was as much nostalgia about this TT as there was about the one the year before: that had been his comeback; this was to be his farewell. The crowds, we were told, would be even greater. It was, after all, a unique chance to see the last race on the island of the most famous name in motorcycle racing history.

But it was an extremely saddened Hailwood who set foot on the Isle of Man on the Sunday afternoon before practice week began. He had been invited as guest of honour to the North-West 200, the ultra-fast race in a triangle over Ulster's northern tip, Coleraine, Portrush, Portstewart – and there Tom Herron had been killed.

Mick Grant, too, had been injured, and it looked as if he was not going to be able to make it to the TT. As it was he bravely shrugged off his pain and took part, but it could only be a token effort in view of the fact he could hardly walk, and for the first part of the week was confined to a wheelchair.

MIKE THE BIKE – AGAIN

Mike recalled: 'I arrived on the island just not wanting to race. Tom's death affected me so strongly. I felt really depressed and I don't suppose I got over the sadness throughout the entire fortnight of the TT. What with him getting killed, and other chaps dying, too, and then Mick's injury, there was a damper over the race from the very start. It was a disaster for racing. Tom was such a marvellous man and a tremendous competitor, and the sport could ill afford to lose men like him.

'It seemed to me that just about every top man in the sport had taken a tumble up to the TT, my time to get going as hard as I could. Every time I opened a paper or looked in on telly there was some leading star going up in the air. And, I must say, it started me thinking. With all of that and my own crash in Italy I was not in the happiest frame of mind ...'

Mike's mood was not lightened when the first practice session had to be called off because of torrential rain and mist that had slashed visibility down to a few yards. Instead, we took out the Mercedes-Benz that Dickie Attwood had loaned us and crept along the circuit trying to find a way through the murk in a bid to get the feel of the place.

Conditions were a whole lot different for Thursday's practice session ... perfect, in fact. And if Mike had any lingering hopes that he might, after all, salvage some vestige of promise from the Ducati for the Formula One race, two days away, they were spectacularly dashed by Scotsman Alex George, the Grand Prix campaigner using the injured Mick Grant's Honda.

For even as Mike was wrestling the Ducati through the twists and turns of the course, George, blistering his hands in hanging onto the breathtakingly quick Japanese machine, was making a mess of his lap record.

An excited gathering of Honda's high officials, every one of them clinging to a stopwatch, stood by the roadside near the grandstand as the flame red Formula One bike hurtled through with Alex George crouched low and determined over the tank. Their heads all went down and when they came up again their faces were split with happy smiles. Within a few minutes their timing was confirmed ...

George had gone round in 20m 12.2s, a lap speed of 112.05mph. Mike's record, set the year before at 110.67mph, had been bettered and George's effort, he claimed, had been minimal. The writing was on the wall for Mike, Ducati and the frantically struggling Sports Motorcycles team. The bike was a hotch-potch – but whatever Steve Wynne tried did not make it go any better and Mike's best F1 time was only 105.88mph. It was so bad that many people, riders among them, thought he was foxing. The only tactic was to try and get them to continue thinking that way so that they might be tricked into breaking their engines trying to get away, when all the time it was not necessary to do so.

In a desperate last throw of the dice Wynne sent away for the 1978 Ducati in the hope that he could cannibalise it and, somehow, build a machine that would do justice to Mike's determination. And throughout

Friday night, with the big race scheduled for the following afternoon, Steve and his men tore apart the so-called new Ducati and started again from scratch using the year-old frame, the new engine, old forks on the back, new on the front. They even cut up an old bedstead from the Palace Hotel – they were garaged in a lock-up behind the Casino – to use for brackets and levers. 'The bedstead special, we called it,' said Pat Slinn, 'and it was just that. But there was nothing else for us to do. We were desperate and so sick at being let down so badly by the Ducati factory. It was amazing to us that Mike was taking it all so well, he could have been forgiven for going up in smoke, the way it was handling. But he was a model of patience, just anxious to help all he could and try to get over to us what the problems were. Any other rider would have gone berserk.'

Mike, who had moved into the house, called to collect me to go to the track. We sat for a while in my hotel, talking over the possibilities and discussing the main dangers to his title. They were all spelt 'Honda', and by Alex George, in particular, for he knew his way around the course as well as anybody. The Honda was the fastest machine in the race, if not the island, and Alex was out to prove himself as a good bet; he had, though it served to make him nervous, an entire range of high-ranking Honda bosses at the TT to watch him. Perhaps, he would have reasoned, this was his biggest chance for a full-time works contract ...

It was to this background that Mike said: 'We haven't a chance today unless something goes wrong with the Honda. I'm so down on power it's embarrassing and the bike is handling as badly as it could.' They were not excuses, they were calm assessments of his chances, and not publicly aired. Few people outside the team realised the difficulties he was facing. He knew, and did not like it, that he would have to try harder than he wanted to ...

The unforgettable finale

Alex George duly won the Formula One race, as expected, and in doing so set up new lap and race records. Mike, in contrast to the heady events of a year ago, struggled home in fifth place.

His best lap had been at 109.39mph, not a significant achievement in itself but enough to stir Pat Slinn to comment: 'That must have been one of his finest ever laps of the TT. On that Ducati, handling as badly as it was and being so way behind in power, it was an heroic performance. I just don't know how he did it; and I'll tell you something more, I wouldn't like to have been the man on it. Only he could have got that thing round at that speed and only he would have kept going as hard as he did. He doesn't know how to quit or how to give anything less than his very best. And what more can you ask? We certainly never expected him to finish so high on the leaderboard.'

The champagne spray was foaming onto the crowd around George, winner by nearly a minute from Charlie Williams on a private Honda, as Mike, who had not even reached his 1978 pace, walked dejectedly away from the celebrations.

He said: 'Well, that's one to forget. I'm bloody glad it's behind me. I tried as hard as I could, but it was pointless. Everything that wasn't wrong at the start went wrong as the race went on.

'I was sure I must have lapped at around 112, the way I was trying. On the old standard of racing measure I was at about nine-tenths all the way, but there was no way I could improve. It seems the harder you try at the TT the worse you are.

'I had a real go from the start, and I mean a real effort. And I was staggered when I got a signal saying something like minus-15 seconds on somebody or other. I was sure I must have been up there with the leaders, it was very frustrating. But it was going the way I had forecast ... Alex romping away. His bike was so much quicker he had only to sit there really. I kept the steam on for the second lap, just hoping for a bit of luck, but after that I thought it would be wiser to cool it and I eased off.'

George's first lap was an eye-opener ... 20m 13.2s, a speed of 111.96mph. Mike's was 20m 49.4s, a speed of 109.06mph. The second time round the Scot had increased to 112.45mph and Mike, still fourth, to 109.38mph. Mike settled for a dice with youngster Ron Haslam, and until he ran into trouble on the last lap, when he was third, the two of them snapped and harried at each other.

'But then I felt something banging against my leg,' said Mike, 'and when I looked down I could see the battery box was swinging loose. I held it in place with my leg until the engine cut out, then I freewheeled for a couple of miles and hopped off to see what was wrong. I found I could get all the wires back in place and, to my surprise, it fired up again even though I had to shove it uphill to start. I was sure I must have slumped back to about fifteenth place – I was stopped for ages – and on the last lap, just after the start-and-finish and with 37 miles to go, I lost top gear. But when I got back to the flag I was fifth. With the problems I'd had I was reasonably happy, though I made up my mind I wasn't going to try as hard as that again.'

He added: 'If anybody thinks I'm going to ride the Ducati in the Classic they're very much mistaken. It's not in the same league as the Suzuki.' The Italians wanted to clear off back to Bologna and had begun to make arrangements, but Steve Wynne wanted to get some sort of return for his investment so he persuaded them that Mike would ride the Ducati in Friday's Classic. But he really wanted the machine for George Fogarty. While it was not perfect it was as good as they were going to get it, and it at least gave George a reasonable mount for the big race. Mike and I went along with the idea – but we told Suzuki's Rex White that it would be with the 500cc that Mike would be tackling the superbikes. He was delighted.

It was close on midnight on Sunday, the night before the Senior race, when Mike and I motored to the garage where the Suzuki was based. The lights were still blazing, and when Mike pushed open the doors he was shocked to see the innards of the 500 scattered like shrapnel on the benches and Martin, Gordon and Dave poring over them. It was evident by their weariness that they had been for some time, too.

Martin said later: 'Mike's face was a picture of gloom. You could see written all over it "Oh, no! Not a Yamaha balls-up." He didn't say it, he didn't have to. We could see the disappointment and the shock were really getting to him. 'What had happened was that we had finished the bike in the afternoon and had fired it up in the lane outside the garage. As soon as it lit up great plumes of smoke began to pour out – it was burning oil. Disaster. And it certainly gave us a big knock-back, we couldn't figure out what could be wrong. But we had to take it down to find out. And we discovered that a coil spring on an oil seal had flicked off. It was a million-to-one chance, in fact I'd never known it happen before. But had he run on it in the race it would not have gone a lap, it was losing so much oil. Can you imagine?

'We stayed up all night getting it right and putting the engine back as it should be. It must have been a bit of a shock to the people in the hotel, because we had to fire it up again at 4 o'clock in the morning. You don't realise what a racket these things make until you start one in the peace and quiet of a hotel grounds before dawn!

MIKE THE BIKE – AGAIN

'We were absolutely beat, we didn't get any sleep at all. Just time to snatch breakfast and get the bike up to the paddock. We certainly didn't feel on top form, and that's so vital when you've got to supervise one of those lightning fuel stops where every microsecond counts. But we expected Mike to be on a peak, so he had every right to expect us to be as well.

'The truth was that the bike we wheeled out for him had not been tried since we had built it up again; we just had to pray we had got it together okay. There was nothing else we could do.'

(Mike did not know it until he reached this point in reading the book that the Suzuki he had for the 1979 TT had a bad history.

The frame was used by Virginia Ferrari when he clinched the West German GP in 1978, ahead of Kenny Roberts and Barry Sheene ...

But the engine was the one used by American Pat Hennen when he crashed at 165mph in the 1978 TT, and then lingered in a worrying coma for three months.

Mike is not superstitious but I would not have wanted to test him on the matter had he known before the race.

Six months after the 1979 TT Suzuki had polished and refurbished the 500cc machine and presented it to Mike as a souvenir. He had wanted the triumphant Ducati the year before – but it was sold to a Japanese collector instead.)

It was a thoughtful, distant Ogborne who blipped the throttle of the Suzuki in the paddock, waiting for Mike to turn up. The machine sounded all right, but was it? Said Mike: 'This is a bit like a journey into the unknown – I'd better take it easy on the first lap.' He looked over at Mick Grant, still suffering from the after-effects of a broken pelvis, only just about managing to walk without the aid of a stick but determined to make sure he gave everybody a hard time in the Senior.

'He must be potty. Look at him, he can hardly walk,' said Mike. 'That first bump at the bottom of Bray Hill is going to be agony for him. He's a brave lad, I hope not too brave for his own good.' Mick was smiling broadly and protesting: 'I'm okay. No problems at all. In fact, it hurts more to talk than to ride. I'm all right when I'm on the bike. And I'll be up there challenging – these guys aren't going to get it all their own way.'

He was as good as his word. He was in front on the first lap with a speed of 111.59mph. Alex George was second at 111.17mph and Mike third at 110.93mph, chased by Charlie Williams at 110.14mph riding a 350cc Yamaha in the shadow of the full 500s. But two laps later Mick's private Suzuki, his own £6,000 investment, broke a crank and forced him out. By then he had slipped back into fourth place, while up front Mike was getting into his stride ...

After lapping at 112.17mph the second time around the six-lap, 226 mile race, Mike peaked to 114.02mph while second-placed Alex George stayed locked on the 112mph mark. On the fourth lap Mike hit

112.06mph, despite a fuel stop, and finished with 112.15mph on lap five and 111.62mph on the final dash.

It was his fourteenth TT win, and he had recaptured all the old flair and dash of his glorious pedigree; he did not rank it level with his 1978 Formula One win in emotional terms, but for sheer professionalism, controlled riding at record speeds, it was a masterpiece. It had gone precisely the way he had planned; the class record of 114.02mph was only 3.2 seconds short of Mick Grant's absolute record, set on a 750cc Kawasaki.

'I didn't think I'd gone so fast,' he said. 'But I'm really pleased to have set that lap record. It shows I haven't lost any of my edge, and after that Formula One disappointment on Saturday I'm happy to be able to show people that I have it in me to go well. I'm sure some of them must have been thinking I'd shot my bolt after last year, and seeing the F1 race ... that's a joke. Race! It certainly wasn't that for me. I was determined to win the Senior: I knew it was my best chance and I made sure I didn't miss out on it. Though I could have done without that scare of the oil leak at the last minute.' Hidden away from the huge crowds, the inevitable following whenever Mike showed his face, in the splendour of the BMW hospitality unit, he swigged a glass of wine and recounted his ride.

'I just burbled round for the first lap, making sure I'd got the feel of the bike and that it was okay. And when I got a signal to say I was 3 seconds adrift of Mick I was reasonably happy and content. I was just about where I wanted to be and setting myself to turn it on a bit, and I felt utterly relaxed and confident. I was certainly well within myself and ready to go. I'd hit the front when I came in for fuel, and that was done in double-quick time by Martin, even though he was bleary-eyed and weary. But I hadn't gone another two miles when I got one of those shocks that always seem to dog you at the TT ...

'The bloody handlebars wouldn't let me turn acute right-hand bends. I didn't know it, but the damper had seized. I just knew I had a problem at the slower, sharper turns. It was okay on the fast bends, the longer swoops, but I had to heel it over and put my feet down to tap-dance my way round on the acute corners.

'And there were three laps left, more than 100 miles. Luckily, I suppose, I was well ahead by then and I was able to knock it off a bit. I'd been giving the bike some stick earlier on, taking it up to ten-and-a-half thousand revs through the gears and eleven thou in top ... about 180-miles-an-hour. But I knocked it back 500 and just tried to make sure I preserved the engine. Even then I got a fright, because it went onto three cylinders and kept cutting in and out all the way home on the last lap.

'Apart from those slight stutters the Suzuki had behaved itself perfectly: I told the lads to give it a quick polish, change the tyres and top up the tank and it'd be just right for the Classic.

'I couldn't find any trace at all of the hinge it was supposed to have in its middle; unlike the 500 Honda I'd ridden in 1967, it handled superbly well and if any circuit is going to find out a fault in handling it's the TT. But

I couldn't have been more satisfied and I looked forward to partnering it in the big race of the week.'

There was £30,000 prize money at stake when Formula One winner Alex George, victor of Saturday's race, faced Mike, the Senior winner, two days later. But neither man, I'm certain, gave a thought to the richest rewards ever in racing in the British Isles; certainly not Mike. He realised, despite his confidence, that it was to be a tough race, the hardest of the week. He did not know just how gruelling it was going to be.

'If I had,' he pointed out, 'I don't think I'd have bothered to turn up. Only once before, when Agostini and I had our tremendous MV-versus-Honda dice in 1967, had I been in a TT as hard. And for an old man like me it was a terrible strain ...'

There could not have been a more apt banner for the last race of Mike's TT career, the Classic. It was just that – and more. A confrontation of such proportion that it defied description, a duel between two men which was a riveting spectacular where the badge of courage shone brightly from each man's chest.

Mike, having carefully charted his pace in the Senior, having balanced it against the effort he'd had to draw upon to stay ahead, knew that the sturdy Suzuki was up to the job he had in store for it. The question was could Mike make up in skill and bravery what the Suzuki lacked in power against Alex George's Honda. It was nearly 500cc down on the mighty, red heavyweight that the Japanese had given the ambitious Scotsman. Mike felt he could; he knew, and so did Alex, that he would be pushing hard into the Honda's engine breaking reserves. He felt, as we breakfasted on the morning of the big showdown, that the Honda might not last the pace he was going to force upon it.

'Alex is good okay, and he's done very well this week, but I can't see the Honda lasting out,' said Mike. 'I'm hoping that will be the ace up my sleeve. It's a long shot, I know, since the Honda is that much bigger , and I'll have my work cut out.'

Not even in my wildest dreams could I have forecast the epic that was to ring the curtain down on the TT – and, of course, on a marvellous career. The 50,000 people who had travelled to the island to witness it were treated to a race that had not been matched for eleven years and probably would not be seen again for twenty.

The splendid fury of it, the blind courage that sent two men tearing into each other's hopes and doubts, the glaring absence of frail fibre on the very threshold of safety and the nerve-wracking tension that invaded every one of the 226 miles of the race served to burn it on to the memory. Mike's stony silence on the way to the circuit, Alex's grim and ashen face when we got there, adequately summed up the mood of both the men. I don't suppose there was anybody who had not worked out that the race would revolve around the number 6 that Mike carried and the number 9 of the Honda.

And that was exactly the way it transpired; poor old Mick Grant tried to push his hurt and injury to the back of his mind. But the pain barrier it left was unbeatable. He was willing enough to tangle with the best in the race he had almost made into his own, but it was not to be in this year, 1979. The improbability of his winning gave way to reality when he had to withdraw from the fray, wincing with the agony of a broken pelvis, saddened and frustrated that matter had won over mind ...

His wife, Carol, and just about everybody who knew Mick and admired his barrel-chested determination, were relieved that he had bowed to the final arbiter ... pain.

Alex had switched to Ron Haslam's bike for the race; he had ridden Mick's in the Formula One event but the Yorkshireman, feeling fit enough to go for the jackpot of the Classic, wanted his own machine back and, being a works rider, had first choice. Mike, of course, was back aboard the one-year-old 500cc Suzuki, the machine he had only ever raced in the Senior. With only ten minutes to go before the race was due to start the Hondas that Mick and Alex were riding were at last fired up, having given their mechanics a shock by refusing steadfastly to start. It took them about fifteen minutes of frantic labour to solve the problem; in the meantime Mike, his stomach churning, his mind a coil of ideas and plans, stood in outward cool shutting out the hurly-burly and rich essences of the warm-up area. It was no time to talk to him – only to shake hands and say briefly: 'See you later. Take it easy – and make sure you get home okay.'

When they fled past the pits the first time round, Mike's red, white and gold image a blur, Alex's four-cylinder, four-stroke engine beating out a triumphant signature tune, the gap was 9.2 secs in favour of the Honda.

Alex had lapped at 112.10mph, a time for the first 37¾ miles of 20m 11.6s. Mike had completed his lap in 20m 20.6s, a speed of 111.26mph. Next was Bill Simpson at 110.70mph and Charlie Williams, on a little 350cc Yamaha, at 109.96 – but there was even better to come from this extremely talented young Cheshireman.

The gap between the pacemakers turned into a tenuous thread. Each man pulled the other into greater effort and lost or gained the advantage in a high-speed gamble of wavering fortunes. In successive laps the space between them was hardly a blink of time ... 4 seconds, 4 seconds again, and 3.4 seconds until it was impossible to anticipate the outcome. Only an outside factor could possibly sabotage the flat-out run for home and glory; and that lay in wait ...

On the second lap Alex went round at 112.74mph, Mike at 112.56mph with Charlie Williams moving higher into the action at 111.14mph, ahead of Bill Simpson at 110. 57mph, Billy Guthrie at 110.44mph and, sixth, Steve Ward lapping at 110.26mph. It was becoming clear to everybody that it was, and would continue to be, a race of fractions of milliseconds.

Lap three – and Alex was still nosing in front with a lap of 113.20mph, Mike at 113.08mph. And Williams had reached even higher on the 350, to 111.28mph, a tremendous performance. On the next circuit Alex lapped at 112.70mph, Mike at 112.62mph and Williams 110.12mph.

Mike, riding as hard as he knew how, made his bid on the last lap but one. And for the first time got the Suzuki ahead of the Honda, but by barely one second. He had lapped at 112.87mph compared with Alex's speed of 112.86mph and Williams' log of 110.04mph. If ever a build-up to a grandstand finish could be seen to be unfolding it was this Classic ...

The two leaders squabbled bitterly, grittily and bravely, over the division of one second. Their prey was a mere fraction of time. Alex opted for a do-or-die bid, and his riding became erratic. He was wide at Creg and too fast, he bumped the wall elsewhere and kicked himself clear, clipped a bank and tested the Honda's braking to the full – but the right hand that was soon to bunch into a fist and wave its triumph stayed twisted round the throttle, demanding all the steam the motor could give him. Mike, too, made a frenzied effort. He rode through the barriers of his own caution, ignoring all the pleas we had made to him before the race, and flew headlong through apprehension, around the very brim of disaster, and swooped, half fearing the outcome had already been decided, across the line. But he had been delayed and diverted off his line by unknowing backmarkers, innocent wreckers of his chances, as he headed to Classic defeat ...

I was waiting at the gates of the avenue that led into the winner's enclosure, so often the stage for his modesty in victory, when he squeezed the brake hard to stop. He hurriedly ripped up the fly-spattered visor and yelled: 'Have I done it?'

'No, Mike, you've lost it by about three seconds,' I answered, 'just three bloody seconds. After all those miles.'

He climbed wearily off the Suzuki that had been such an eager partner, his face a mask of disappointment. 'Oh Jesus, and I tried so hard. So hard. I was sticking my neck out all over the place, far more than I wanted to. But I really wanted to win this one. I tell you what, I wouldn't want to go through a last lap like that one all over again. I can't imagine what Alex must have been riding like ... I know I was pretty near the limit. Then I came up against some backmarkers who were wandering about all over the place and that slowed me up. Probably lost me the race. But it's not their fault.' It was the first time he had been second in a TT.

The last lap had been a sensation of action. Alex had done it in 19m 49.6s, a speed of 114.18mph. Mike's time was 19m 53.8s. His speed: 113.77mph. And Alex had won the race by 3.4 seconds, in the fastest time in the 72-year history of the TT.

It was an extremely disappointed Mike who strode the length of the finishing avenue, cheered all the way by fans who knew they would never see his like again.

As we walked he was full of self-recriminations. He said to me: 'I was over-confident. I thought I could do it; I should have tried harder, particularly early on. But I didn't believe the Honda would go so far so fast. I have only myself to blame, but I wish I'd have tried a bit more.' It was a mood that passed as quickly as a fleeting cloud as soon as he saw Alex; he was generous in his praise, genuine in his admiration. They were emotions that were returned wherever he went, for every action of Mike's sincerity evokes a reaction of increasing admiration.

At a party later that night his fun was infectious. He had raced his last TT, a 21-year courtship with the island's whims and vagaries had come to a rather magnificent finale. There were joke bluebottles dropped in strangers' drinks, a close group of friends to share the feeling of relief that he was, indeed, bringing an end to the most prestigious racing career of them all. That he would no longer feel the need to shoulder responsibility and polish the gloss of the legend he had created for himself while being embarrassed at every minute of the public recognition that went with it.

It is remarkably easy to eulogise Stanley Michael Bailey Hailwood, George Medallist and MBE, but terribly difficult to rationalise, when you have been so close for such a long time and watched even the greatest achievements being dismissed with infuriating modesty. His TT comeback in 1978 and his farewell in 1979 gave him joy and tears, rapture and disappointment, but they gave him the chance to show his genius, too, to many thousands of people who found that the myth of the man could be recaptured and repeated.

Fame has an uneasy perch on his shoulders, crowds of admirers terrify him, and praise to his face often shocks and embarrasses him fearfully. The fact that he was a TT lifesaver for two unforgettable years only leaves him with the worry about who will follow him into that role.

Vernon Cooper, the man who is the power behind road racing in the United Kingdom, the brains behind the TT, a hope for its future and the authority with whom I worked for Mike's comeback, made a telling summing up of his value to the race for two years.

'When we shook hands on Mike's comeback, it was probably the most important symbolic gesture in the long history of the races,' he said.

I told this to Mike at our soiree after the Classic and, as usual, he tried to find a route around the compliment. He came up with the answer: 'Well, it did me a favour, too. I got a second place, I've never had one on the island before.'

In his case, he does not have to race to be a winner.

Postscript

Pauline
by Ted Macauley

Triumph and tragedy are emotions and experiences that can test resilience and resistance to often unimaginable degrees. They dwell in starkly contrasting effect in the likelihood that they may intrude on the lives of the most unsuspecting of people.

And that is what happened to Mike. In devastating contrast to his triumphant TT return came his tragic death, along with that of his nine-year-old daughter, Michelle; the result of a truck driver's carelessness in unexpectedly turning into Mike's car on a main carriageway. The errant trucker was taken to court and fined.

It is impossible to imagine the shock and resultant ongoing heartbreak and shock for Mike's wife, Pauline, when she lost her much-loved husband and beautiful daughter. From my own point of view Mike was my best friend, and hardly a day passes without my having a thought of him. How Pauline has coped is a tribute to her inner strength, and love and loyalty for an extra-special being.

Pauline revealed her deepest thoughts in a moving interview she gave me, to be used in the national newspaper I wrote for then as the Chief Sports feature columnist. And I am moved to return to it ...

This is a re-run of my article which appeared under the headline 'Life Without Mike.'

'Her sadness sometimes shows in her bright blue eyes, and at times, she still seems stunned by despair.

'Pauline Hailwood, at 37, is a beautiful woman who is trying to adjust to a life without her husband, Mike. He was the greatest of motorcycle racers the world is ever likely to see: a man who, for 24 years, staked his life on his skill only to be killed, along with his nine-year-old daughter, in a road crash that was no fault of his.

'He put his courage on show and won the George Medal for it. Now it is Pauline's turn to be brave – but all she can win is an elusive peace of mind.

'She sits in her comfy lounge behind the latticed windows of the home she and Mike shared in a village outside Birmingham, where he had set up a motorcycle sales business, and says: "I went to a film show that was all about Mike. It was the first time since he was killed that I have seen him moving and talking.

"It was a weird experience and it took all my best effort not to cry out. But in one sense it helped to keep him alive in my mind and in my heart. Everywhere I go in the house ... our lovely home ... there is some reminder of him, some treasured little memory – and they all help to keep me sane. I have changed nothing. I have kept the house just as it was the day he and Michelle went out and never came back. I just cannot understand people who throw away everything ... the clothes ... the pictures ... the souvenirs ... all the wonderful reminders ... and try to wipe out the precious memory of somebody they loved, treasured and admired so dearly. For me, it is just as if he has gone off racing somewhere, and will be away for a little while.

"That is what I keep telling myself, not expecting him to walk through the door because he is out of the country racing. That way, it will gradually become normal for me to realise he is never coming home."

'She cuddles her son, David, the seven-year-old who survived the horrible crash without injury.

"It all happened a while ago, but David still has nightmares about it. He never talks about it when he is awake. But I hear him jabbering away when he is asleep, so obviously his mind is still in turmoil.

"He staggered me one day when he suddenly asked me why I don't get married again. And when I asked why, he said he wanted another daddy. And I had to explain as best I could that I still loved his daddy very much, and that I could not possibly love anybody else, and he would have to make do with me. But I can see he is being very brave and he misses Mike and Michelle terribly.

"Mike was such a lovely man. I used to look at him and think that he cannot be the same guy who has done all those incredibly brave things all his adult and professional life, spent right on the very edge of survival at terrifying speeds, wheel-to-wheel with equally committed riders. He was like a man with two identities. One at home ... loving ... a devoted family man who doted on me and his two children ... just happy to be domesticated and a daddy and hubby. The other fellow was a devil-may-care star ... a hero to millions of people all over the world ... the dashing and heroic Englishman everybody loves to love and worship and admire.

"It is the HERO that everybody knows. But to me he was just my HUSBAND. He was just a nice guy to live with, the finest of men to have children with, and with nothing showing on the surface that had you believing or realising that he was a legend who had really achieved all those incredible triumphs and world titles ... and with such overwhelming modesty."

'Pauline, whose face and figure clinched her glamour roles in British movies and earned her big money as a fashion model, tries hard to deaden her grievous sense of loss. She pauses to gather her thoughts, and wonders if she should reveal her big secret.

MIKE THE BIKE – AGAIN

"I have never told anybody this, but a few years ago I went to a palmist for a look into the future. Mike would have scoffed at the very idea, but I sneaked along without his knowing. And the palmist told me that in 1974 I would have a great moment of joy – and one of sadness.

"Well, David was born in May. Then in August Mike had a terrible car crash racing in the West German Grand Prix at the Nürburgring, and it bloody near killed him. He was badly hurt and was left with a limp for the rest of his life. Then I remembered later she had told me that the man I loved would go out of my life in my thirty-sixth or thirty-seventh year.

"When Mike made that fantastic comeback to racing at the top level in the Isle of Man TT in 1978, and then again in 1979, I lived with this awful dread. I didn't dare tell him. I figured he had enough to think about – but I lived on pins while he was racing around the world's most dangerous circuit, the scene of so many tragic crashes and rider deaths.

"When he finally decided to quit racing altogether, having won twice on his comebacks at the TT, I still kept my little secret. The danger, as far as I could see, had passed. He had survived all those years and fooled the forecasting palmist.

"Who could ever have believed she was right all the time? Certainly not me. And just when I thought we could settle down to a life without risk at long last he goes and gets killed in circumstances over which, ironically and tragically, he had no control. But I would bet, typically, he fought like a bloody demon, right until his last breath, the very last moment of his life. It had to be something way beyond his control to end his life. Nothing else could have. Not if he had anything to say or do about it."

'There is another pause and Pauline says finally: "That old lady future teller did have one more forecast. She said I would remarry in my early forties. How wrong could she be? Nobody could replace a man like Mike. Never."'

Appendix

1978 Formula One TT Results

Position	Number	Competitor	Machine	Time (h:min:sec)	Speed (mph)
1	0	Mike Hailwood	Ducati	2:05:10.2	108.51
2	0	John Williams	Honda	2:07:09.6	106.81
3	0	Ian Richards	Kawasaki	2:08:07.6	106.01
4	0	Helmut Dahne	Honda	2:08:26.8	105.74
5	0	Alex George	Triumph	2:08:28.2	105.72
6	0	Chas Mortimer	Suzuki	2:10:50.4	103.81
7	0	Malcolm Lucas	BSA	2:12:00.4	102.89
8	0	Kevin Wrettom	Kawasaki	2:12:03.2	102.85
9	0	Denis Casement	Honda	2:13:26.6	101.78
10	0	Ian Tomkinson	Triumph	2:14:16.6	101.15
11	0	Asa Moyce	Kawasaki	2:15:05.4	100.54
12	0	Charlie Sanby	Moto Guzzi	2:16:00.0	99.87
13	0	Ray Knight	Dresda Honda	2:17:49.4	98.55
14	0	Doug Lunn	Fraser Ducati	2:20:28.4	96.69
15	0	John Williams	Honda	2:20:33.6	96.63
16	0	David Cartwright	Ducati	2:23:03.8	94.94
17	0	John Wilkinson	Suzuki	2:23:14.0	94.83
18	0	Max Nothinger	Kawasaki	2:23:49.0	94.44
19	0	Frank Rutter	Robinson Triumph	2:24:58.2	93.69
20	0	Barry Roberts	Laverda	2:24:59.2	93.68
21	0	John Hammond	Moto Guzzi	2:26:20.0	92.82
22	0	Dennis Trollope	Yamaha	2:26:46.0	92.54
23	0	Dennis McMillan	P & M Ongar Kawasaki	2:27:03.2	92.36
24	0	Graham Bentman	BMW	2:27:21.2	92.17
25	0	Harold Gasse	Suzuki	2:27:43.8	91.94
26	0	Peter Davies	Laverda	2:27:52.0	91.85
27	0	Neil Tuxworth	Honda	2:31:13.0	89.82
28	0	Peter Taylor	P & M Kawasaki	2:39:09.2	85.34
29	0	Thomas Willison	Kawasaki	2:43:48.0	83.42
30	0	Barry Homewood	Rickman Kawasaki	2:46:11.6	83.11
31	0	Nev Watts	Yamaha	2:53:29.2	78.74
DNF	0	Hartley Kerner	Dresda Honda	–	0
DNF	0	Guy Sandall	P & M Kawasaki	–	0
DNF	0	Phil Read	Honda	–	0
DNF	0	Joey Dunlop	Honda	–	0
DNF	0	Peter Lovell	P & M Suzuki	–	0

MIKE THE BIKE – AGAIN

Position	Number	Competitor	Machine	Time (hr:min:sec)	Speed (mph)
DNF	0	Les Trotter	Crooks Suzuki	–	0
DNF	0	Roger Bowler	Honda	–	0
DNF	0	Michael Hunt	Laverda	–	0
DNF	0	Eddie Roberts	Ducati	–	0
DNF	0	Tom Loughridge	Crooks Suzuki	–	0
DNF	0	Dave Kerby	Norton	–	0
DNF	0	Tom Herron	Mocheck Honda	–	0
DNF	0	W A 'Bill' Smith	Yoshimura Bimota Suzuki	–	0
DNF	0	Roger Corbett	Triumph	–	0
DNF	0	Mick Poxon	Triumph	–	0
DNF	0	Ron Haslam	Honda	–	0
DNF	0	Jim Scaysbrook	Ducati	–	0
DNF	0	Roy Jeffreys	Honda	–	0
DNF	0	Roger Taylor	Laverda	–	0
DNF	0	Geoff Kelly	Laverda	–	0
DNF	0	John Stephens	Honda	–	0
DNF	0	Roy Armstrong	Moto Guzzi	–	0
DNF	0	Martin Russell	Rustler BSA	–	0
DNF	0	Jack Higham	Hall Honda	–	0
DNF	0	Jim Rae	Ducati	–	0
DNF	0	Mal Kirwan	Suzuki	–	0
DNF	0	Roger Nicholls	Unknown	–	0
DNF	0	Ewan McKechnie	Unknown	–	0
DNF	0	Jan Strijbis	Unknown	–	0
DNF	0	George Fogarty	Unknown	–	0
DNF	0	John Crick	Unknown	–	0
DNF	0	John Caffrey	Unknown	–	0

1979 Senior TT Results

1	0	Mike Hailwood	Suzuki	2:01:32.4	111.75
2	0	Tony Rutter	Suzuki	2:03:39.4	109.84
3	0	Denis Ireland	Suzuki	2:04:07.2	109.43
4	0	Steve Ward	Suzuki	2:04:59.0	108.63
5	0	Steve Tonkin	Yamaha	2:06:23.2	107.67
6	0	Chas Mortimer	Yamaha	2:06:46.4	107.14
7	0	Ian Richards	Yamaha	2:07:47.8	106.28
8	0	Kenny Blake	Yamaha	2:08:02.4	106.08
9	0	Bernard Murray	Yamaha	2:08:09.0	105.99
10	0	Bill Ingram	Yamaha	2:08:35.0	105.63
11	0	Steve Cull	Yamaha	2:10:36.0	104

Position	Number	Competitor	Machine	Time (h:min:sec)	Speed (mph)
12	0	Derek Randall	Suzuki	2:11:41.0	103.14
13	0	Hans–Otto Butenuth	Suzuki	2:12:26.6	102.55
14	0	Ron Jones	Suzuki	2:12:31.6	102.49
15	0	Mick Chatterton	Maxton Yamaha	2:12:46.2	102.3
16	0	Les Trotter	Crooks Yamaha	2:12:48.0	102.28
17	0	Alan Jackson jnr	Suzuki	2:12:58.2	102.14
18	0	John Stone	Yamaha	2:13:16.8	101.94
19	0	Neil Tuxworth	HLS Suzuki	2:13:38.0	101.64
20	0	Alan T Lawton	Yamaha	2:13:56.4	101.41
21	0	Malcolm Lucas	Yamaha	2:14:51.0	100.32
22	0	Graeme McGregor	Yamaha	2:15:27.0	100.27
23	0	Nigel Rigg	Yamaha	2:15:37.2	100.15
24	0	John Long	Yamaha	2:17:48.0	98.56
25	0	Derek Huxley	Spondon Yamaha	2:19:48.4	97.15
26	0	David Goodfellow	Maxton Yamaha	2:20:13.4	96.86
27	0	Denis Casement	Yamaha	2:20:59.8	96.33
28	0	Keith Buckley	Yamaha	2:21:19.6	96.1
29	0	Bill Tomlinson	Yamaha	2:24:01.8	94.3
30	0	Charlie Williams	Yamaha	2:28:53.2	94.22
31	0	Tom Loughridge	Yamaha	2:29:12.6	90.22
32	0	David Greenwood	Yamaha	2:29:55.2	90.6
33	0	Chris Bond	Yamaha	2:32:06.2	89.38
34	0	Walter Dawson	Yamaha	2:36:32.2	86.33
35	0	Derek Wood	Yamaha	2:36:45.8	86.04
36	0	Wolfgang Wilhelm	WW Yamaha	2:39:18.0	85.26
37	0	C Neve	Yamaha	2:42:09.0	83.26
DNF	0	Billy Guthrie	Suzuki	–	0
DNF	0	Peter Labuschagne	Meadspeed Yamaha	–	0
DNF	0	Bryan Robson	Yamaha	–	0
DNF	0	John Weeden	Yamaha	–	0
DNF	0	Eddie Roberts	Maxton Yamaha	–	0
DNF	0	Mike Duncan	Yamaha	–	0
DNF	0	Mick Higgins	Suzuki	–	0
DNF	0	Alex George	Cagiva	–	0
DNF	0	Derek Chatterton	Chat Yamaha	–	0
DNF	0	David Hughes	Matchless	–	0
DNF	0	Bill Fulton	Maxton Yamaha	–	0
DNF	0	Vaughan Coburn	Yamaha	–	0
DNF	0	Ernie Coates	Yamaha	–	0
DNF	0	John Taylor	Yamaha	–	0
DNF	0	Kwong King Wong	Suzuki	–	0

MIKE THE BIKE – AGAIN

Position	Number	Competitor	Machine	Time (h:min:sec)	Speed (mph)
DNF	0	Kevin Wrettom	Suzuki	–	0
DNF	0	Steve Moynihan	Yamaha	–	0
DNF	0	Kenny Harrison	Yamaha	–	0
DNF	0	Ken Inwood	Yamaha	–	0
DNF	0	Mal Kirwan	Sarronset Yamaha	–	0
DNF	0	Mick Grant	Suzuki	–	0
DNF	0	Ron Haslam	Yamaha	–	0
DNF	0	Joey Dunlop	Suzuki	–	0
DNF	0	Bill Bowman	WLT Yamaha	–	0
DNF	0	Martin Hall	Yamaha	–	0
DNF	0	Hubertus Weber	Yamaha	–	0
DNF	0	Bill Barker	Honda	–	0
DNF	0	Dennis Trollope	Fowler Yamaha	–	0
DNF	0	Roger Nicholls	Yamaha	–	0
DNF	0	Ricky Burrows	Suzuki	–	0
DNF	0	Bill Simpson	Suzuki	–	0
DNF	0	Roger Wilson	Yamaha	–	0
DNF	0	Sam McClements	Ryan Norton	–	0
DNF	0	Noel Clegg	Yamaha	–	0
DNF	0	George Fogarty	Unknown	–	0
DNF	0	W A 'Bill' Smith	Unknown	–	0
DNF	0	Brian Peters	Unknown	–	0
DNF	0	Barry Smith	Unknown	–	0
DNF	0	Herbert Schiefrecke	Unknown	–	0
DNF	0	Greg Barsdorf	Unknown	–	0
DNF	0	Peter Groves	Unknown	–	0
DNF	0	John Cousin	Unknown	–	0
DNF	0	Derek Loan	Unknown	–	0

ACKNOWLEDGMENTS

My grateful thanks for the valued contributions, encouragement, enthusiasm, and generous interest of: twice world Superbike champion and gifted musician, James Toseland; legendary broadcaster Murray Walker; great friend, F1 mastermind, and motorcycle racing fanatic, Bernie Ecclestone; F1 genius Sir Jackie Stewart; John Watterson; Stuart Barker at Virgin Media; Ellen van den Berg at Lookwell Adrian Ashurst for his photographic expertise, attitude under pressure, and constant support; and Sports Motorcycles supremo, Steve Wynne, for taking the chance on Mike.

Also from Veloce Publishing ...

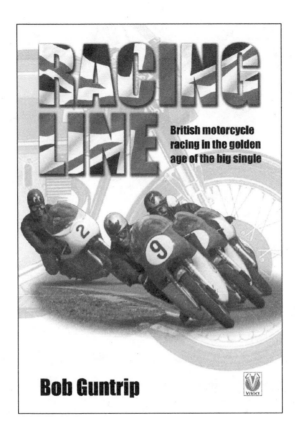

Racing Line is the story of big-bike racing in Britain
during the 1960s – when the British racing single
reached its peak; when exciting racing unfolded
at circuits across the land every summer; and when
Britain took its last great generation of riding talent and
engineering skill to the world.

V4793 • Hardback • 22.5x15.2cm • 232 pages • 76 colour and b&w pictures
• ISBN: 978-1-845847-93-7 • UPC: 6-36847-04793-1

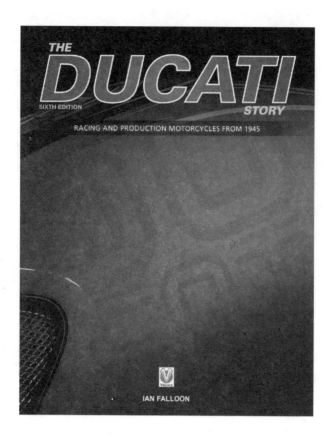

Ian Falloon's authoritative history of the marque –
expanded and brought up to date for this 6th edition
– tells the inside story of Ducati's chequered path to
glory, and describes every model, from the original
48cc Cucciolo to today's exotic Superbikes.

V5085 • Hardback • 27x21cm • 368 pages • 349 pictures
• ISBN: 978-1-787110-85-4 • UPC: 6-36847-01085-0